Getting the
Right
Job

Judy Skeats

WARD LOCK

A CASSELL BOOK

This edition published in the UK 1995
by Cassell plc
Wellington House
125 Strand
LONDON
WC2R 0BB

Copyright © Templar Publishing Company Ltd, 1989 and 1995

First published 1989

Distributed in Australia
by Capricorn Link (Australia) Pty Ltd
2/13 Carrington Road, Castle Hill NSW 2154

A British Library Cataloguing in Publication Data block for
this book may be obtained from the British Library

ISBN 0 7063 7429 0
Typeset by Servis Filmsetting Limited and
The Templar Company plc
Printed and bound in Great Britain

Contents

1. Introduction

There is no magic formula for job hunting, but by approaching it methodically and following some basic rules, you will vastly improve your chances of success. Each chapter of this book can be read alone, but your job hunting will be more effective if the book is read sequentially. Working through each section will help to give you a thorough understanding of what you want, why you want it and what you need to do to succeed. For those who find it difficult to stick to this, some important advice has been repeated in later sections, where appropriate.

Who is it aimed at?

The information in this book is designed to help job seekers of all kinds, from school or college leavers and the unemployed, to those returning to work or seeking a career change. The aim is to help you analyse yourself and put forward the best interpretation of your skills and experience for each job. As the interviewing process should comprise a relatively small part of the job-hunting process, there is a large amount of space devoted to helping you find the *right* job – making sure that you can get to the interview stage and that the job you are pursuing is one that you will be happy with. The book, therefore, shows you how to prepare for all aspects of job hunting, how to put together your Curriculum Vitae (CV) and what sort of information you should arm yourself with as well as giving you pointers on how to conduct yourself at the interview.

What do you want?

One of the cornerstones of job hunting is analysing what you want. This is essential for your future satisfaction – there is no point in wasting time in applications for a job or career, only to discover some time later that this really doesn't suit you. Also, unless you have really understood what a job entails it is very difficult to gear your application towards it, as you will not know which factors are particularly important to stress. You may also find that potential employers will reject your application, having seen your limited understanding. In other words, you must know what is involved. Trained interviewers are used to spotting works of fiction!

This book will help you to analyse the skills and experience which you already have and to present these effectively to prospective employers. It does not attempt to give extensive careers advice. If you need this, or are not completely sure of what you want, you should clarify your aspirations before embarking on the search for your ideal job. Advice of this sort can be gained through Jobcentres, privately run careers agencies or by reading careers handbooks. Some advice on good careers guides is given at the end of this book, although this is not exhaustive.

This book assumes that you are applying for jobs within the United Kingdom. If this is not the case, seek further guidance on local customs in the countries you are interested in. You may not need to address the potential employer in his/her native language but you will have to ensure that you say the kind of things that they will want to hear, that is, using appropriate forms of expression.

Sell your skills

This book aims to help you to market yourself successfully. The chapters take you through the process from beginning to end, from deciding what you want, drawing up your CV, attending the interview and then deciding if you want the job. The books also helps you analyse your CV and/or interview performance if you are not offered the interview or the job. There may be several reasons for this, and careful analysis, along with the feedback you will have collected will help you plan your next, successful, attempt.

Whatever your chosen profession or career, you will have to sell your skills and sell yourself. Job hunting is an exercise in persuasion in various stages – you must prove to the potential employer that you can do the job, do it well and will be better than other applicants. Competitiveness in the labour market means that employers are increasingly discerning, so it is essential to have a good CV and interview style as well as the skills that the employer is looking for. All interviewers recognise that they are taking a risk in employing people. You must convince them that with you the risk is minimal.

Aim to sell one thing at a time; the CV and initial letter or application form should gain you an invitation to an interview. The interview should lead either to a second interview or directly to an offer of a job. Take each step at a time; you may appear over-keen or desperate if you ask directly for a job at the first application stage. The appearance of desperation is to be avoided at all costs. If you appear over-anxious to gain a job, the interviewer may well wonder what is wrong with you and why you have not been snapped up by another organisation. This may seem grossly unfair, but it is important. Many interviewers *do* think that way and you will benefit by recognising this.

The book focuses on the importance of role play, that is, practising the interview before you attend. It is important that you are able to put forward well-thought-out arguments, expressed confidently, but without sounding pat. The interview is a one-off situation – you don't get a second attempt at the same thing – so it is important that your responses are right first time.

Keeping records

Although this may sound dull, effective record keeping will help you in your search for the right job. It doesn't have to be extensive, but you should keep a list of the jobs you have applied for, the date of your application, when you received an acknowledgement, interview dates and the response. Together with the latter, you can keep a note of the reasons why you think you were successful or not (remember you may not choose to accept every job offer, but you should know the reasons why you declined).

Keeping records will help you if you wish to apply for another job with a company to whom you have made an application in the past. The information you gathered on that previous occasion need not be duplicated (though you may wish to check that it is still up-to-date and compare with any later developments), and having this will save you time.

Keeping copies of your application together with the advertisement and any information on the organisation will also help you recap before the interview. If you are making several job applications, it can otherwise be difficult to remember what you said to each employer, particularly if this was for different types of work or the applications were submitted some time ago. You must be able to remember the criteria which you had decided were important and why.

Allow enough time

Job hunting takes time. It is important that you do not rush the stages of this. An employer must be shown your best efforts rather than scribbled notes or shoddy presentation style. If you aim to convince potential employers that you are worth their effort, both in interviewing you and subsequent induction and training, they deserve this. Remember that other applicants will be spending time to get this right. If you want to give yourself a fair chance, you must do this too.

The methodical approach will help to prune preparation time, but guard against overdoing this. Thinking time is important too, and, as you will discover, you may need to prepare slightly different applications for different posts and take time understanding the culture of the organisation so that you will be accepted by it. This latter point is an important one – interviewers want to ensure not only that you can perform in the job, but that you will not be disruptive to other staff. That means that you must be seen to be able to accept those values that are the norm within the organisation.

Reading this book should help you to gain a better understanding of what you want and how you fit into the labour market. Good luck in your job hunting!

2. Before applying

What kind of job do you want?

It is very important that you analyse the type of work you want to do, so that you can apply for the things that you are going to enjoy. If you are in a position where you need to apply for any job which you can do, rather than waiting for one which you would *like* to do, the same basic guidelines apply. You will need to know what your priorities are – interviewers may be able to spot an application where your heart isn't in it. If you are unsure whether you want the job or not, this may be one of your potential weaknesses and knowing this will forearm you for situations where the interviewer may be cynical.

It is very important in a job application that you angle your experience to suit the job. You will be able to do this much more effectively if you know exactly what you want and what the potential employer wants. This means that as well as knowing yourself, you must find out what the employer is looking for and what the job really entails. Only then will you be in a position to know which posts you can realistically apply for.

If you know what kind of job you want to do, this is half the battle. You will also need to know what kind of organisation you would like to work for (this will be explored later). However, if you are unsure of where your skills lie, or what you would be good at, you should analyse this before you begin to make applications for jobs. Nobody else can tell you what to look for, and aspects of the job or company which are ideal for one person may not suit another at all.

Adding up your past experiences and your preferences for the future must be done individually for each person by themselves. Part of this process will be sorting yourself out!

In many cases careers advice is limited, or difficult to obtain (and this is true not just for those approaching their first job, but also for anyone changing career). There are many things that you can do to help yourself in this, as well as finding professional careers advice. There are various books and courses which can help you work out what kind of work you would prefer and what other factors influence this. For example, you may find that your skills naturally lie in selling, but you are not able to be mobile. Although this may limit your range of potential applications, it should not prevent a sales career.

Analyse your skills

Most careers advice focuses on analysis of your skills, often through various tests of your aptitudes, and also takes account of your preferences. You will need to capitalise on the skills you have and decide whether you need further training in any area. You should also focus on your likes and dislikes, your preferred working style, whether you like to work alone or as part of a team, etc. Ask yourself questions such as, are you happy leading a team? How much support do you want? Are you self-motivated or do you like to have your tasks set for you? Do you prefer routine work where you know exactly what you are doing, or do you like the challenge of trying new things? Do you prefer work that requires attention to detail or the ability to take a broad overview, and which are you good at? All these factors can help you make decisions about what is right for you.

If you have already had some work experience, try to think back to the specific parts of it which you enjoyed or disliked. Think about the sort of people you prefer to mix with too. Many tests used by career analysts and careers guidance organisations measure whether your main motivations are for achievements, where you need to be in a framework where you can obtain definable successes; for affiliation, where you would like to be in surroundings where you get on well with the people around you; or for power, where you need to be able to influence the tasks or people around you. If you know your own views of these things, this will help.

There are of course, many other factors which you will wish to take into consideration. If you have not thought through this process, then find a good careers book to give you some guidance (there are a few listed at the back of this book).

You may find it a useful exercise to write down all the things you are good at and when you last used those skills. Include everything at this stage, you can screen out anything which is not relevant later. Note what your bosses or teachers have said that you were good or bad at, and include all non-work achievements. Don't forget to add the unusual things that you have not done for a while as these still might be useful if they guide you towards your aptitudes. Include popularity or similar attributes – these are not worthless and could point you in the direction of a career, anything from reception work to PR!

Once you have finished this exercise, go through your notes to see if any pattern emerges. Ask other people to look at your list too, as they may see aspects which you have not spotted.

Where do you want to work?

There are other aspects to consider once you have decided what sort of work you are looking for. Although the function of the job may be similar from place to place, you will find different emphases depending on whether you are considering a large or a small company.

Large organisations may have better security and fringe benefits but may be more bureaucratic. You may find that because they need a lot of people in each discipline, the work is more specialised (as nobody would have time to cover the whole of that subject area). Conversely, a small company may leave you more autonomy and freedom of action and the opportunities to widen your experience across a broader range in your job. However, the 'perks' may not be as great.

You will have to weigh up your needs and desires for support, training, promotion, prospects for variety of work or sophistication of work, so that you know what balance will be right for you at this time of your life. It also pays to think ahead; which will be better on your curriculum vitae in the future? How marketable will you be to future employers once you have gained sufficient experience in the job you now wish to apply for? Other aspects of the organisation which you may wish to consider may include the amount of structure. Some people feel much more comfortable when they know exactly what the rules are, others like less-defined, flexible frameworks.

Making your skills/experience fit your future career

Once you have considered all these factors, and any others which are pertinent to you, then you can look at your past experience and the skills you have acquired to see whether they fit. You must recognise mutually exclusive desires, for example, high-powered jobs and lots of leisure time – you may read lots of stories about people doing business on the golf course, but it rarely happens when you are starting out!

You may find it helpful to draw up a chart showing the job you want, and the skills and experience you think would be required alongside your own past achievements. Ask friends and family to help you if you are unsure. If you are able to chat to anyone already doing the kind of job you want, this will be very helpful. See what their careers background consists of and whether this is a normal pattern or not.

It is important that you are relatively clear about the job content of your chosen position. Although there will always be factors about the job that you cannot know in advance, you should find out enough to convince yourself that your picture is realistic. This is valuable, not only for forestalling disappointment and disillusion if you take up the job, but also, in order that you may angle your experience to the job effectively. Interviewers will be much more impressed by candidates who have done their homework and know what is involved.

By assessing the job (some guidance on how to 'read' the advertisement is given in the next chapter) and your own potential, you will be saving yourself time by not applying for posts which are unsuitable. It can be very demoralising to keep applying and being turned down without knowing why. Don't do that to yourself! A little initial work and forethought will help to save you from this.

Find your 'bottom lines'

All this will give you a broad idea of what you are seeking. Now you should work out your 'bottom lines', that is, those factors which you will not compromise on. These may be financial needs, or a limit on travelling distance, etc., as well as some aspect of the work itself.

Bottom lines may include salary and working conditions – work out your financial needs by calculating what you need to spend each week/month and then add 10 per cent for the things you'll forget! If you are using your previous (or present) salary as a guide, don't forget any bonus entitlement, etc. You may also wish to put in a figure for savings or holiday money. Your holiday entitlement may be important, pension arrangements, or ability to have lunch provided. Or you may just know that you only work effectively if you are in nice surroundings. All these things should be taken into account. Work out your ideal and then which ones you can afford to compromise on, or which ones you would give up in return for other specific benefits.

Check out the level of the job, in terms of the hierarchy or seniority. Look at the percentage of the work you can do easily against that which will present a new challenge. Believe in yourself – you probably have a greater ability to take on new things than you realise, many people have.

The list below gives some ideas of things which you

will need to consider before making an application:

Salary and monetary elements

This may include basic salary or wages, bonuses, profit shares or overtime payments. You may wish to check whether you will have to ask for an increase or whether rises are automatic and if so, when. In some cases the advantages of a good initial salary may be offset if you later slip behind other companies in the industry for some reason. Find out whether the organisation has a policy to pay people well, or as little as it can get away with! (The next chapter will help with this.)

Look also at the pension arrangements and the amount of the employer's contributions. Do you gain life assurance or sickness benefit? Is membership of a private healthcare scheme included? Does the organisation offer any financial (or other) assistance with relocation? There may also be provision for a company car; if so, you should check on the amount of tax which you will be liable for. There may be expenses paid at flat rates for travelling on company business, so think about the implications of this.

The job itself

Most organisations provide job descriptions or at least a rough guide of what the job entails. If the organisation is expanding or declining, this may be subject to change as the job may grow or contract. Finding out the size of the job is important – some organisations expect their staff to take on a lot of work, and/or get involved in everything from doing the accounts to cleaning the floor, depending on what is needed at the time.

It will benefit you to know what the organisation expects. In addition, one of your questions at an interview may be to ask the employer to describe a typical day. It can be very difficult otherwise to gauge what is really involved. Also, find out how much supervision will be given as this is an indicator of your autonomy, and what support will be given, either by colleagues, subordinates or others.

Working conditions

This will include everything from the surroundings to the number of hours worked per day. Find out if overtime is expected or usual. Find out whether you will be sharing a large or a small office or have one to yourself. If your chosen job is not office-based, what will your base be like? How much travelling will there be? Will you have to stay away from home on business? Is there an initial training course which you will have to go away for?

The organisation

Assess the organisational culture to find out whether you would be happy working there. There are many aspects to this and it can encompass points such as the usual range of backgrounds of the staff (are they all graduates, etc?), the amount of bureaucracy and control imposed (relative freedom can mean that you aren't quite sure what you are supposed to be doing) and the effort expected or pressure of the organisation, etc. Company literature will help you assess this and there are also some pointers in the next chapter. However, it is important that you decide what you want and assess the advantages and disadvantages of the different organisations you are interested in – recognising the impact of these factors on you.

Promotion prospects

Look at the future prospects both within and external to any company you are considering applying to. For example, you may consider taking a post with a company known for its good training, in the knowledge that you will be sought after by other organisations in the future.

The track records of other people in your department will be useful pointers. Find out what the promotions policy is. Remember that few companies will paint a very gloomy picture of this, so you may have to weigh this up alongside other information you have gained about the company to assess this properly. Small organisations or those with decreasing market shares may be able to offer less, although this may be offset by other factors.

Once you have thought through all these various factors, write down what the ideal would be in each of the circumstances (keep this realistic though, the object is not to fantasise, but to be constructive!). Then work out what your most basic requirement is. This should represent your bottom line – the factors which you will not drop below, or give up. An example of this is given overleaf, 'Ideal' is followed by 'bottom line' in italics.

Ideal and *bottom line*

Salary c. £17,000
Salary c. £15,000 with pension

Company car and other benefits
Mileage allowance, sick scheme

Own office, secretary
Own office, shared secretary

Modern spacious surroundings
Surroundings unimportant

Job offers training and promotion
Job offers some training

Large organisation with sophisticated systems
Organisation can provide some new experience

3. Understanding the advertisement

In order to marry your own skills with those required for the job, and angle your experience successfully, you must analyse the advertisement. This means looking at both the explicit requirements and those which are implicit.

There are many things that you will need to look for in the advertisement and many of these just need common sense. Once you have started to analyse these, you will be able to draw your own conclusions without difficulty. Analysis will fall into one of three categories, the organisation, the job itself and the qualities required of the individual who will perform the job. Some examples of advertisements and how they can be analysed are given towards the end of this chapter.

Once you have decided what is important to you about the job, you will know what to look for first; for example if travelling or relocation is not a problem you might look first at the job title, whereas, if you are not able to be mobile, the location may be your first concern. Alternatively, you may have decided that the important thing for you is the culture and size of the company or the training that you will receive.

Where is the advertisement?

The media used gives you an idea of how much the company is prepared to spend on advertising to find the right person – local papers are less expensive than the nationals or the trade magazines. There may be other reasons for choosing that medium though. Organisations tend to use local newspapers where they do not expect applicants for that type of job to travel far – perhaps for more junior posts. Alternatively, they may expect a large response so do not wish to 'widen the net' further than the local community.

National newspapers and trade magazines or journals are more expensive. The national press has a very wide readership, so the chances are that the organisation will receive a large number of replies to the advertisement. This is, of course, what they are seeking, but also means that the competition can be stiffer! Companies may advertise in these because they know that they will reach individuals with the qualifications or experience they seek and/or if they expect to receive replies from all over the country. This is particularly true when they are attempting to find well-qualified staff where there is a skills shortage in their industry.

Advertising in the national press may also indicate a prestige post. For each advertisement, ask yourself whether the company would have to advertise there (is this the only real source of specialists?) or whether there would have been alternatives. For some types of work, advertising in the trade journals may be the only real way of reaching the right readership.

Where companies seek many people, for example, if a new production plant is opening, they may also advertise on local radio. Usually these 'spots' are short but tell anyone interested where to find the written advertisements which they may be interested in.

The newspapers used may also give an indication of the politics of the organisation. Certain newspapers have come to be associated with broad political viewpoints and the firm will want to ensure, as far as possible, that as well as giving a good spread of applicants, they will be like-minded and will fit in with the company culture.

The appearance of the advertisement

The shape and design of the advertisement can tell you a lot about the company. If the advertisement is well put together – not squashed into too tight a space and with a clear logo or company symbol – you can assume that advertising is usual for the organisation. This may not necessarily be recruitment advertising, but many organisations will use this medium as well as their product advertisements as a public-relations tool. It is another opportunity for them to show the public their business and extol its virtues.

The large boxed advertisements are of course more expensive than the lineage. Design for the style of the advert can be expensive too, but many companies believe that this is important in order to preserve their corporate image and show a consistency with other sides of the business.

In general, the larger the advertisement, the more important the post. If the company is spending a lot on finding the right applicant, they want to believe that they will be worth it, particularly if they are also likely to spend a lot in training the individual. Recruitment costs can be high for the organisation – remember that they not only have to pay for the advertisement, but also to give some induction (or initial) training to familiarise the new employee with 'the ropes'. This takes time and perhaps lost opportunities in sales, etc., for the people doing the training, so it is important for them that they get this right. Nowadays companies cannot afford to take on someone who '*might do*', it's just too expensive in terms of lost time.

The style of the advertisement will give you information about the company too, not just in what it says about itself (and that is of course very important) but in terms of whether it appears to be a modern or old-fashioned company. Is the narrative boringly written? What kinds of words does it use? Those advertisements noting a *dynamic, fast-moving company* are likely to give you a very different impression to those which note that they have a *long-established record of success* and denote more traditional ways of working.

The organisation

There are many things to note about the organisation. Note whether the company is large or small, expanding or stable (very few will admit to contracting in size!) Is it a well-known name? If so, you may find that it does not need to say very much about itself (although in practice, a large number of companies want to remind readers at every opportunity that they are the market leader, etc.). Lesser organisations may need to explain their products or service further – often you may have heard of the product but not realised who made it.

Is the wording formal or informal? This gives an indication of the culture and whether the company is likely to be bureaucratic or fast moving and relatively unstructured. Some companies advertising nationally make a virtue of the location, particularly if it is difficult to make people move there! For some new towns, the amenities may be very good, but the organisation will be aware that most people have not realised its full potential yet and that they need to convince the reader. (Naturally this kind of explanation will be omitted from local papers when the readers already know the good and bad points about the area.)

Look at the subtext if there is one, such as the slogan that the organisation uses along with its name. This will show if the focus of the company is on quality of the product, customer care, etc. These are usually short slogans such as *a great name in . . .* , or *quality is our commitment.* They may be specific to the industry, for example, a delivery service that says *we'll get it there*, or a razor manufacturer who says *we have the cutting edge.* These subtexts tell you not only what the company does but how it does it, or thinks it does it. (Some other examples of these are shown in the advertisements later in this chapter.) Remember that the organisation is telling you what it perceives itself to be and to do. Your impression may be different, but it is important to note what *they* pride themselves on.

If the company says that it is expanding, there may be opportunities for promotions in the future. Sometimes they will also say that the last job holder has been promoted. Expanding companies, or those with fast-moving markets often recruit individuals who can give them real commitment in terms of hard and effective working. Expectations are high both from the company and the individual. In some cases 'flexible working' will be expected, where everyone is expected to pitch in to get the job done, whether the tasks come within the job description or not. Also, companies may describe themselves as entrepreneurial or FMCG (fast moving consumer goods).

Note that 'young companies' may be operating an age bar, so that only young individuals will be taken on. Conversely, other advertisements may say that applicants under a certain age are unlikely to have obtained the experience required for the post. Also, look for equal opportunity statements and no-smoking policies, etc., as an indication of company style.

Box numbers

In some cases, the company will not give its name but will advertise under a box number, so that this will remain confidential until they write back to you. This is unusual as most companies do not want to give the impression that they are ashamed of themselves! They are often used in unusual circumstances, for instance if a company is considering moving but not all its employees have been told – omitting the company name, therefore, is often viewed with suspicion! However, there are other less sinister circumstances when box numbers are used, such as companies which are just launching themselves in a highly competitive market – obviously they do not wish all their competitors to get to know all about them!

Who do you reply to?

This is a useful clue to the organisational culture. Formal organisations may ask you to respond in writing to Mr or Mrs X, or even more formally just give the person's title. Informal ones may prefer *call Sally on* . . ., etc. Those organisations which are large and therefore recruit many people may ask for responses to be sent to the recruitment manager.

Sometimes respondents are asked to reply by telephone – the organisation has committed itself to time to talk to all the callers. In many cases, the person you have to call will be able to give quite a lot of information about the job and the company but they are also likely to interview you there and then, on the telephone. You may of course be asked for a further face-to-face interview once they have decided that your skills are appropriate. For posts involving a lot of telephone work or needing a good speaking voice, this kind of screening is useful to the employer.

Those organisations asking you to reply on their application form are likely to have a more structured approach than those requesting just a copy of your CV. This is often true of employers advertising themselves as equal opportunity employers – they are keen to compare like with like, avoiding bias and gathering all the information they think will be useful, rather than finding many differently presented CVs which can be more difficult to compare.

If there is a job reference, there may be many posts advertised and employers often use different references on different advertisements so that they can find out which paper or journal produced most responses.

Agencies

If the recruitment is being undertaken by an agency, this may be to save the employer time. Small employers like using the expertise of professional recruitment agencies, who often conduct the first round of interviews and some testing of the candidates. Large employers may use agencies to save time for their busy personnel departments, particularly if they have a hectic recruitment campaign running or if they require recruitment in a new area.

Agencies can become involved in varying degrees, ranging from designing and booking the advertisements to shortlisting and screening potential employees. For the potential employee the process may be longer if they have to attend first an interview with an agency and then a further appointment with the company itself. Note that agencies often charge a minimum of 17–20 per cent of the successful applicant's annual salary, so the company are investing heavily in this process.

The job itself

Look at the job title. In some instances these can vary greatly for the same job depending on the organisation. A typist in one company may be called a secretary in another, etc. The secretarial field is particularly prone to this and the text in the advertisement should make it clear whether the company is actually looking for a typist, secretary or PA. The job titles 'Officer' and 'Manager' also often mean different things in different places.

A good advertisement should give a clear idea of the duties to be performed. It should be the bait which makes you more interested in the organisation and therefore makes you apply. Larger, more structured organisations will provide a job description; in new or smaller companies where the job itself is less well defined, there may be more flexibility. Also, the more senior the post, the more difficult it would be to describe each task involved, and applicants would be expected to know from their past experience what they would need, in order to undertake the job.

The advertisement may give clues as to how you would interact with others, saying *working on your own initiative* or *working as part of a team*, etc. With the former, there is likely to be less direct supervision so that the job holder has the ability to decide for him/herself what is important. Team working would indicate more day-to-day contact with others, possibly on a shared task, and you may be required to be able to 'fit in' more readily.

Look for phrases such as *good sense of humour needed, ability to withstand pressure* or *ambitious self-starter*. These indicate varying amounts of pressure. Although some people want to work with others who share their sense of humour, those who state it as a requirement are likely to do so only if it is really needed. If you enjoy working under pressure, it may still be worth finding out what kind of pressure the organisation means as this can vary in extent and type. The phrase, *ambitious self-starter* usually indicates pressure as well as a lack of direct supervision and the *challenge* referred to in many advertisements usually goes hand-in-hand with hard work.

If the job needs good communication skills, you will have to be very careful to demonstrate these on your application and at an interview. This is where assessing yourself is particularly important because it is relatively easy for the potential employer to spot this if you don't have them!

In some cases, the employer will say that the right person is more important than previous experience. This usually means that the job can become whatever you want to make it (within reason!) and that the employer is looking for a certain personality to sell his/

her products or to merge successfully into the company. In some cases, there is a commitment to provide the required training for the job. Note though that the phrase *young person required, will train* often means a low salary if the organisation can't afford the more experienced, trained person!

Boring jobs may be jazzed up with exciting phrases, particularly in industries which sound glamorous. There are always many people trying to find work in the film industry, arts administration, in advertising or the music world, etc., and some companies exploit this by making it the main feature of the advertisement even though the job only involves copy typing, etc.

The phrase *attention to detail* denotes the meticulous approach needed and this may be repetitive. Watch out for those advertisements indicating a low boredom threshold. Even worse! Look for any signs that the job has been oversold, which could denote that the employer is promising something that cannot be delivered as part of this job.

Look for mobility clauses too. Sometimes it will be obvious that travelling will be an integral part of the job, in other cases, it may be implied by references to a full, clean driving licence. Posts requiring HGV licences may also involve helping to load and unload the vehicles.

Sometimes the employer also states certain personal characteristics which he/she thinks are desirable. On other occasions this may be implied, for instance, it is unlikely that the company would agree that a shy, retiring introvert would make a very good salesperson. On the other hand, imaginative, extrovert airline pilots may be frowned upon! Think about whether you have the qualities requested and also how you can demonstrate these either on the application form or at an interview.

Most of all, remember that the employer is likely to list all the qualities that he/she is looking for, in other words, those that they would find in an ideal candidate. They seldom expect to find the perfect employee, however, and you must assess which criteria you think are essential and which are desirable, but not imperative. Try to see the job from the employer's angle and work out what you think will be crucial. If you have the chance to ask others in the industry or check with careers advisers, etc., this will be very helpful.

Qualifications and experience

In some cases the exact requirements will be stated. In others, these will be left to your own discretion. Sometimes a range of qualifications or experience would be equally suitable and the employer merely states that *appropriately qualified individuals* are sought. There may be legal minimal for the post which anyone in the field would know of, for example, solicitors must be qualified and anyone working in that field would know of this.

Some employers find it easier to specify certain basic qualifications rather than think about whether these are really needed. Or, they may ask for five 'O' levels because they always have done – however, you have to take a calculated risk if you choose to ignore this. As a general rule you should assume that as the employer knows more about the job than you do, they know why they are asking for the particular skills they are requesting. There are a few exceptions, though.

If qualifications or experience are requested, but you know that your qualification/background is just as good, it may be worth applying. For instance, a company asking for GCSE French would presumably be equally pleased to find an employee who did not have the qualification but spoke and wrote the language fluently. (Don't bluff though, you may have to demonstrate this!) Always make sure that you have a valid case before applying – try to think about why the advertiser has requested these skills or qualifications before making the application. For example, even if you think that speedwriting is just as good as shorthand, it may not be useful to the employer if somebody else has to read it back. Also, if formal external training is to be given, employers may request certain qualifications because they will afford the individual's entry to the course needed.

Prospects

These may be stated within the advertisement if there is a clear career path. However, check what is the norm for that particular company if you can, or at least find out the most usual career structures within the industry as a whole. Although many organisations wish to promote from within, they do like to think that you will stay a reasonable time in your first job, so be careful about being too pushy. Naturally, if the advertisement states that they require someone ambitious, you can play up this side.

Salary, terms and conditions

The exact starting salary for the job is not always

quoted. However, the salary or wages are usually quoted clearly at the top of the advertisement when they are especially good.

In some cases a salary range is given and it is usually safe to assume that you will have to start near the bottom. However, you may find that there are additions to the basic wage, consisting of city weighting allowances (in London this is often divided into Inner and Outer London Weighting Allowance) or shift premiums, overtime payments, etc. Where overtime payments are made, it is usually wise to discover in advance whether overtime working is compulsory or not. There may also be other bonuses or commissions added to the basic salary, sometimes depending directly on your performance in the job.

Salary ranges are usual in the public sector, which tends to be clearer about finances than the private sector. Beware of advertisements saying *up to* . . . unless you are very confident of your own marketability – the figure catches your eye but it is often not apparent what the minimum salary for that post is.

Euphemisms such as *attractive salary package, the right rewards for the right people, salary will not be a problem for the right person* or *salary commensurate with age and experience* often show that there is no fixed bottom salary. These are often seen in industries where salaries are secret and other employees do not know what their colleagues earn. These slogans usually mean that the salary will be negotiable.

Circa or *c.* on an advertisement, before a salary figure, means that the salary is *around* that particular level. As a general rule, assume that you will not be able to achieve an increase on the basic salary above 10 per cent.

High commissions paid are often linked to low basic salaries, particularly in sales posts, where the commission is a direct incentive to achieving higher sales. In this type of work you may also see catch phrases showing how much top sales people (usually called consultants in these advertisements) earned last year. Advertisements sometimes begin *do you really want to be rich?* and go on to tell you how you can do this with their company, usually saying something along the lines that most people are too busy earning a living to make a fortune! Unless you know that you too can be a top salesperson, assume that you will not achieve this!

Attractive salary package may indicate that taken together, the financial rewards are good. This may include relocation payments/assistance, and fringe benefits such as a good pension scheme, life assurance and health insurance, company car, luncheon vouchers or discounts on company goods, etc. (Where benefits of the job are itemised, they are usually set and not open to negotiation.) Alternatively, the employer may concentrate on future promotion prospects and the greater financial rewards there.

If no salary is quoted, this does not automatically mean that the level will be low. For some vacant positions, the company will be famous enough to attract high calibre applicants without stating the salary, and often the organisation simply wants to check out the commitment to them. In some cases, it is part of the industry's culture not to quote salaries as these vary greatly depending on the experience brought in by the successful applicants.

If an hourly wage is quoted, make sure you know how many hours per week you will be required to work as this could make a great difference to the final, weekly pay cheque. In some companies, employees and workers are entitled to a paid lunch break, but this is not always the case.

Some examples of advertisements:

```
PSV
DRIVERS

Small, expanding coach
company in East London are
looking for experienced Class 2
and 3 PSV Drivers.

We offer a good salary and a
job packed with variety.

PHONE 01-... .... NOW
```

This is a small, unsophisticated organisation which has the capacity to grow. As they are looking for several Public Service Vehicle drivers, it is likely that they have already made a good name for themselves locally and have attracted several orders to help their expansion. As the job is to be *packed with variety* the reader can assume that there are several different 'buyers' for the services of this company, giving different kinds of work.

The organisation has not yet developed a 'corporate image' for itself and omits its name. Perhaps it can't handle any more work at the moment, until new drivers have been recruited! Also note that there is not a name for respondents to contact.

The small size and lack of explanation about the job or terms and conditions suggests that the company is new and that everything will be explained to enquirers in person. Anyone applying would already know what is mainly required, from the request for Class 2 and 3 licences.

In the advertisement on the right, the organisation is luring those who want to share its success. Found in the local paper, it aims to entice individuals who can be trained. All they need apart from knowledge of personal computers and accurate typing is a good telephone manner.

The *drive and determination* suggests that this will be hard work and the emphasis on the success of the company indicates that mistakes are not allowed! The exact salary is not shown and may be low at first but there is the promise of promotion and a real career structure. The *personality* part suggests that individuals should be outgoing and able to chat easily to strangers over the telephone, perhaps pacifying them if their parcels go astray!

The advertisement is well designed and the slogan indicates that the aim of the organisation is to 'do it better than you could yourself!' The company is proud of itself and its achievements and will strive to safeguard its reputation for excellence, reliability and customer satisfaction.

CUSTOMER SERVICE
• *A world of opportunity* •

ABOUT US

Parcels Direct is a highly successful transnational parcel delivery service. With an unmatched record of reliability and innovation in Canada, we are now bringing our expertise and unique business approach to the European market.

ABOUT YOU

Our new headquarters in Basingstoke will be the focus of our European operation. We now need bright Customer Service Clerks with the ambition and commitment to build an exciting career on our worldwide success.

You will be an important part of the team – responsible for tracking parcel deliveries throughout Europe. Previous PC experience and accurate typing are essential, but we are looking for more – the personality to liaise with clients on the telephone plus drive and determination.

We offer a highly competitive salary and benefits package, together with the opportunity to further your career in a company which genuinely rewards success.

To apply, please telephone Jane Smith on...................... or write to her enclosing your CV (Address)

(Parcels Direct logo)

Better than taking it there yourself!

BUYING
The essential ingredient

Fantasy of Life makes fine fragrances which are truly individual. Each character in our range has undoubted style and elegance. Our company has an established reputation and a sophisticated clientele.

Now we need an experienced buyer to undertake this growing load alongside a key staff member who will shortly be retiring. Your excellent skills will include accurate purchasing and inventory records (computerised or manual) and the track record of purchasing raw materials at advantageous prices in addition to your outstanding negotiating and communicating abilities.

We offer a very competitive salary, pension scheme, life assurance and all the usual benefits of a successful international company.

Please contact Mrs. Gibson . . . .

Another company proud of its reputation, and with the glamorous touch. The bait is the perfume, but the job could be buying any of the raw materials, or even the office furniture! The advertisement is fairly traditionally written and may be old fashioned in some ways – it indicates that individuals stay until retiring age and stresses accuracy and track record; all solid, reliable skills.

There may be a sharp divide between the high-profile perfume sales side and the back-room functions. The communication and negotiating side may give evidence of more excitement, however.

No details of the salary are given. Perhaps this is a trade secret! Also, there is no indication from the advertisement of the size of the unit, and whether this is part of the head office or a satellite. As it was advertised in a local paper, however, the organisation may rely on the fact that it is well-known in the area.

4. Other ways of finding out about vacant jobs

There are many ways, other than through press advertisements, that employers advertise their vacant posts or methods that you can find out about them. These include finding advertisements through agencies, using networks and people you know, PER, Jobcentres and jobclubs, 'jobs vacant' notices outside the organisation's premises, the 'milk round' and job fairs, etc., as well as writing speculative letters enquiring whether the organisation has any suitable vacancies.

Employment agencies

There are several different kinds of agencies which can help you find a job. Employment agencies include the 'high street' agencies which often deal with both temporary and permanent positions. These usually advertise a selection of their better jobs on boards at the front of the premises to tempt passers by. Employers may approach the agency asking for their help in filling the vacancy or the agency may approach them if they have seen the post advertised and believe that they have the candidate to fill it.

Specialist agencies exist covering different types of work. The most well-known are the secretarial and clerical agencies (which tend to be the 'drop in' variety), but many others exist covering areas such as finance and accounts, engineering, nursing, graduate recruitment, public relations and various specialist branches of management. You may have to write to some of these; most of them advertise in the trade press or the favourite media for individuals with those skills.

Good agencies will discuss with you in depth what you are looking for and what your skills are so that they can give a true picture to the prospective employer. It is important for their own reputations that they only refer those candidates who are able to do the job and who fit any other requirements. Employers use agencies to cut down the workload so that they do the initial sift of applicants and turn down the 'no hopers'; that is those candidates whose skills and experience do not match what is required. They can then interview the good candidates themselves.

Sometimes an agency will attempt to talk an employer into interviewing a candidate they feel to be particularly suitable, even though there may not be a complete match with skills and experience. In these cases, it is the agencies who have been reliable in the past from the employer's point of view who succeed.

It is important that you treat the agencies with respect. You should send or take a good copy of your curriculum vitae to them and make sure that you are smartly dressed when you meet the personnel there. It is wise to think of agencies as prospective employers because until you convince them of your worth, you cannot get to the employer. They act as a middle person between the employer and you. Make sure this is not a barrier! Remember that the agency may also be referring other individuals on their books to the organisation. Their prime objective is to find an individual from their 'pool' to fill the job, which does not necessarily mean you. You may, therefore, have to keep contacting them, so that your card does not find itself at the bottom of the pile. It pays to nag a little!

The high street agencies have many vacancies to fill and will be performing a juggling act between pleasing the client and pleasing you – remember that the client pays the bills though! The agency may suggest a number of options or possible jobs for which they could put you forward. Often, if you are visiting their office, they will telephone the prospective employer there and then to see whether they can get you an interview. Usually they will agree to keep in touch with you and if the first batch of jobs is not suitable they will ring you when something else arises. In some cases they will be advised of vacant posts before they are advertised or the client may prefer to allow them to handle it all rather than advertising at all.

Typically these high street agencies also have many temporary posts on their books too.

Recruitment agencies

Recruitment agencies are slightly different from employment agencies. They may take on varying amounts of the work from the personnel department of an organisation. This may include as little as designing and placing the advertisements or may also include replying to applicants and drawing up the shortlist for interview. In some cases the agency also conducts the first interviews for the client company.

You will have to reply to most recruitment agencies by letter (send a CV too as most agencies do not have application forms), very few are geared up for 'drop in' visitors in the same way as employment agencies, so you will then have to make an appointment to see them. Again, if interviewed by a recruitment agency you must convince them in the same way as an employer. For you, as the potential employee, this is a double hurdle and the interview time will be increased as you must attend an interview with both the agency and the organisation itself. However, if you get to the interview with the company you will know that you stand a good chance of being offered the post.

Recruitment agencies are less likely to keep comprehensive lists of candidates. They are primarily interested in filling the vacancy that they have been contracted to fill. However, there is still a chance that if the job you were originally interested in has been filled already, or you are not successful, they may have others which would be suitable.

If you see a general advertisement for an agency suggesting that you could find something suitable, make sure you enclose a list of any organisations for which you do *not* want to work.

Headhunters

Most people are not likely to encounter headhunters, who approach individuals directly rather than waiting for the individual to approach them. Headhunters are typically employed by the organisation to find suitable candidates for high-powered vacancies. They seek out suitably qualified people who have made a name for themselves and who might want to move on to something else if the package was good enough. (They think in terms of 'packages' because salary is often not the most important thing to people who already earn a lot of money and are looking for tax-efficient ways of increasing their overall renumeration.) Headhunters tend to be used only for very important posts or those that are difficult to fill and their fees can be very high indeed.

Headhunters operate by knowing their specialist area and having contacts who are experts in the field. These contacts may be asked if they are interested in the post the headhunters are trying to fill for their client. Or, in turn, they may know of someone else who is suitable. Naturally, in order to do this, the headhunters have to be fully in touch with what is happening in many organisations and/or have effective networks of people whose opinions and recommendations are respected and reliable.

Using networks

This is just a case of utilising the people you know both within your own area of work and socially. if you are seeking a new job, you can make this known to other people. Also, listen when they talk about their workplaces as you may be fortunate enough to hear early news about possibly vacancies arising.

Initially, this is a very informal route; although once your interest is established and the employer has decided to see you, if may progress exactly like any other job application. The main difference is that you have been pro-active in finding out about it.

If you have not yet found your network, you can do this by studying the kind of industry/area of work that you are seeking. Make a few appointments to chat to people who you think can give you good advice (but do not ask them for work directly, as they may well be put off by this and not help you). Find out whether there is any existing network. Many professions and vocations have established groupings of people, either through professional associations or groups that have just emerged as other people's needs have required. Find out what people in those areas of work typically read; there may be useful advertisements for networks and meetings in the appropriate journals.

Although networks can be a good source of finding jobs, their primary aim is to swap useful information to assist people in their jobs. For example, personnel specialists may meet to swap information about salaries and fringe benefits. These may be confidential and the group exists on the basis of trust. Other areas such as sales and marketing may be more difficult for an outsider to infiltrate, as the subject matter can be more sensitive. There is a growing number of professional networks and many geared specifically towards women too.

You will help yourself within the networks if you are a good self-publicist (but not too immodest!) as you will need to make people remember you and what you are good at. You must not appear too pushy though and should take an interest in the primary function of the network, rather than obviously being there only to make contacts to find a job. (Remember that all the information you gather here will help you in your application though, it is definitely not wasted.)

PER

Professional and Executive Recruitment Limited is an agency offering a comprehensive range of services to job seekers on a national basis. Registration with PER is free and can be accomplished by sending a CV or requesting an Application Form from their Sheffield office: Professional and Executive Recruitment, 631 Chesterfield Road, Sheffield, S8 0RX.

Details of each candidate are held on a central computer. When a client vacancy occurs, PER search their files for suitable candidates.

Candidates are always notified before their details are given to the company. PER will set up interviews and ensure that each candidate is well informed about the company offering the vacancy.

PER offer a career counselling service, Curriculum Vitae Service and do personality profiles.

They also offer temporary or contract work opportunities for registered candidates.

Jobcentres and jobclubs

Jobcentres are run by the Department of Employment and can be found in most towns. They tend to advertise jobs which are local and usually focus on those which do not require many qualifications. Any employer can give them a list of their vacancies. The Jobcentre does not charge for displaying details of these and they can be readily seen by anyone who walks in. Jobcentres operate in the same way as employment agencies. If you are interested in something displayed on the boards, you can ask for more details and the Jobcentre will attempt to make an appointment for you to see the employer.

Jobclubs are run for individuals who have been unemployed for some while and these will give advice on how to apply for jobs, help people draft letters of application, provide postage stamps, etc. They often provide telephones and give support to help people avoid the depression and despair that can be felt after a number of applications have been turned down, or if there are few posts in the area to apply for. Both

Jobcentres and Jobclubs can also arrange to provide careers advice for individuals who need it.

Vacancy notices

Some organisations will display a list of their vacancies outside the premises giving details of who you should apply to. Generally these just give the job title or the kind of work, such as, *Fitters wanted – apply within* without any details. The person you speak to should therefore be prepared to give you all the details you need to know and will not necessarily expect you to have done any research about the company.

This method tends to be used only for jobs where the requirements of the job would be obvious to anyone applying and where suitably qualified individuals would be found walking past. Using the fitters example again, a fitter will know what he/she does and what qualifications or experience is required. Specialist, technical and managerial posts are seldom advertised in this way.

The 'milk round'

This is a process by which organisations, who take on a number of graduates, travel round to various universities and colleges to talk about the company and interview prospective employees. In many cases they have a graduate-trainee programme where new graduates are taken on and then given spells in different parts of the company, learning all the various different functions, before they choose which they are to specialise in. Job offers may, however, be conditional on the individual passing the degree and/or gaining a certain class within that.

The milk round is mainly undertaken by large traditional organisations who employ a large number of staff, and may take on hundreds of graduate trainees per year. The travel and time involved is not cost effective for those employing only a small number of people.

Job fairs

Increasingly, job fairs are becoming popular. These are exhibitions for employers to display their glossy literature about their organisation and chat informally to anyone who might be interested in working for them. These are similar to the milk round system, but are not limited to university graduates. Indeed, many polytechnics are arranging them for their Diploma students, etc., as well as undergraduates.

Smaller or representative organisations, as well as the larger employers, are often invited to have 'stands' or 'stalls' where they will provide details of what working for them would involve. In some cases they may not be recruiting many people but wish to raise general awareness about their company and possibly to take the first steps towards recruiting future staff for the next year.

Speculative letters

Speculative letters are those which are sent to prospective employers that you have identified. These organisations are those that you have picked out as preferred employers, even if they are not advertising any jobs vacant at that time. You simply write to them asking if they would consider you for any suitable vacancies now or in the future. These letters should be sent with an accompanying CV.

Your imagination may be caught by an advertisement where you know that your skills and experience do not match the requirements of the job but you like the sound of the organisation, Or you may have prepared a list of all the local organisations noting which you might like to work for. In both these cases you can send a speculative letter. This should explain briefly why you would like to work for the organisation, what kind of work you are looking for and a little about your skills, experience and background (not too much because your CV should give all the main details).

The purpose of this letter is to introduce you, so the points in the letter should be well thought out and aimed at the kind of job that you want. They should synthesise the points in your CV which would be important for this job and this company. Do *not* waffle; the letter must be short and succinct. Each point must relate specifically to something that will be relevant to the organisation. Keep things simple and don't gush! You can state *I am good at . . .* rather than *Mr. Bloggs, my last employer thought that I was the best person he'd ever had doing x and he'd seen a lot of different people . . .*

You should send a letter because this will give all the information you wish to impart. Telephone calls can be more difficult as you will not necessarily know if you have got through to the decision maker and it is difficult to convey the same amount of information in a structured way.

Make sure that you write on A4 paper (not highly coloured) and avoid sending heaps of examples of your work! (If necessary and appropriate say that examples can be provided.) Make sure that your letter and CV are well presented without spelling errors and most importantly, tell the reader what you want and expect (*see also* the section covering CVs). Many people write good letters about their experience and skills but fail to show what they are looking for – and it isn't always obvious, so make sure you do not forget this bit. You must decide whether you want to ask if the organisation has any suitable posts now (but bear in mind that they are not advertising) or whether it would be sufficient to be 'kept on file'. Always ask for what you want.

Remember the rules of letterwriting; a letter beginning *Dear Mr Smith* ends with *Your sincerely* and one beginning *Dear Sir* ends with *Yours faithfully*, etc. If you are not sure about this, look it up. (*See also* the chapter on application forms and accompanying letters.) Ideally you should find out the name of the person you will be writing to and you can find this out by telephoning the organisation.

5. Preparing your CV – the basics

CV stands for Curriculum Vitae, a Latin phrase which literally means 'the course of (one's) life'. It should describe the events of your life which are important to the potential employer. CVs are sometimes referred to as resumés, particularly in the United States and Canada.

The golden rule is that you should be able to talk about whatever you include in your CV and to elaborate on it. This means that you must keep the bluff to a minimum! Angling the experience to fit the job and weighting the emphases does not mean that you can create a work of fiction.

Whilst the details in your CV must be true, there is no reason why you should not have several versions giving different emphases so that each is aimed at a particular type of job. You should remember that other applicants may well have access to word processors, etc., so that they can produce a CV which is modelled on the specific job that they are aiming for. You must make sure that you can match the opposition!

If presentation and spacing are important, brevity is crucial. Make sure that your CV does not run on longer than three pages at the most. (Academics may be the exception to this rule.) The CV should be easily readable and the spelling and grammar *must* be correct. Ask a friend for help on this if you think this might be difficult. Ambiguity must be avoided too. Because you may inadvertently write something which is not clear, it is useful to obtain the opinion of a friend. It is particularly easy to lose clarity with regard to your work experience because you are so familiar with it. Do not assume knowledge of the business when explaining the facts to an outsider.

The basic details which you should include are:

- personal details
- education and qualifications
- work experience and career history
- personal interests, hobbies and pastimes
- other relevant details for the job such as driving licence, languages, computer skills, etc.

Personal details

This section should include your name, address and telephone number (if applicable), and can also include other factors. Make sure that your name is at the top; you may want to add a note of your sex too if this is not immediately clear from your name. The address should be clear and should be the one you wish to have your correspondence sent to – do not put in your home address whilst you are at college during term time! You can avoid this by including in your covering letter (there should always be a covering letter with a CV) details of both addresses and the dates you will be at each. (This is rather lengthy to put in the CV itself.) Remembering to add the postcode may mean that a response reaches you faster.

Your title does not need to be included on the CV if it appears on the covering letter. Other items commonly included under this section are date of birth, age, marital status, dependant children, nationality and business telephone number.

In general, unless the employer will need these details at the outset, avoid them. Date of birth may be useful (remember to put in the correct year and not the year in which you are writing – a very common mistake!), but entries for marital status and dependant children take up valuable space on the paper and the employer does not need this information in order to decide whether or not you can do the job applied for. Nationality may be something that you wish to include if you have a work permit (which should be stated) and you should only give your business telephone number if you are able to be contacted there and can talk without being overheard or interrupted. If you have a home telephone with an answerphone, it is useful to say so, but again, if you are short of space on the CV, put this on your letterhead of the covering missive, including your STD code.

If, however, you do have lengthy, pertinent details which *must* be included, you do not need to put these at the beginning. You want the employer to read through the CV and they should, therefore, be able to see the 'interesting bits' at a glance, preferably on the front page. If these details take up a lot of room, you can simply put the name, address and telephone number at the beginning and put other details in the section containing personal interests and hobbies at the end. This way you will gain more prime-position space in which to place the important things which will convince your prospective employer of your worthiness for the post.

Whatever you feel is necessary to include, however, you should use your imagination with the layout, so that the design not only saves space but shows more thought on the presentation. Your CV should be designed to make an impact, though without being completely zany! If your CV is likely to arrive with many others, you must make every effort to ensure that it will be noticed. In the example below the relevant, fundamental facts are clearly presented and maximise on the use of available space:

SALLY SMITHSON
43 Tudor Road
Off Cheltenham Drive
West Wetteringham
Gloucestershire   Wetteringham (01667) 584141
G34 P25   Date of birth: 14.7.69

Another example, though less space saving, experiments with type size:

SALLY SMITHSON

●

43 Tudor Road
Off Cheltenham Drive, West Wetteringham
Gloucestershire
Wetteringham (01667) 584141

Date of birth: 14 July 1969

In the first example, the date of birth was described only in figures. To avoid confusion, particularly if you are applying to North American or European companies whose conventions are different, it is sensible to put the month in words.

Education and qualifications

Traditionally, this section followed that describing personal details. However, increasingly this is being placed after the work-experience section, particularly if any qualifications were completed long ago! Unless you are a school/college leaver or an academic, the work experience may be more relevant.

With this information you can either put the two together or split the qualifications from the educational establishment (if indeed, you wish to put the latter in at all). This may be done so that the qualifications are clear and well-spaced rather than jumbled up together with other information. It is also advisable to list them in reverse order so that the highest qualification is read by the prospecitve employer first. Make sure it is prominent. He/she may have only a marginal interest in your 'O' levels or GCSE if your degree is highly relevant.

As a general rule, it is unnecessary to give details of the grades of the basic qualifications but the class of degree might be helpful, providing it was a good one (if not leave it out!). If you have quoted grades of your qualifications, make sure that you give them all. The reader will notice if you have included only the good ones!

If you have taken exams but failed them, use your discretion on whether to include them or not. In the case of one failed exam among many, it may not be necessary or appropriate to put this in. However, if you have spent several years studying for a qualification which you did not attain, you should include this or it will leave a gap in time, something which always arouses suspicion and irritates the reader! Do not go into great detail about the reasons why you failed, particularly if it was a long time ago, but if there is a sound reason which you can express succinctly, you may wish to do so. If you did not finish the course and therefore did not sit the examinations, you can simply state *course discontinued.*

Remember to insert the dates for this section, but do not put in your infant or primary school as only relevant data should be included. If your senior school is likely to impress, put it in, if not and you will need the extra space to describe something more relevant to the reader, leave it out. Make sure that anything you include will be understandable to the employer. If your most recent qualifications are unusual or taken overseas, for example, it would be helpful to note their equivalent level here.

Employment history or career progression

Make sure that you devote the most space to the most relevant (usually the last) job. It is useful to show your employment experience in reverse chronological order, that is, your last job described first. This is because it is the main one you want the employer to pay attention to. If the reader has many CVs to look at, you will not want him/her merely to glance over your CV and miss the most important part because it was right at the end.

It is particularly important with this section to adapt the descriptions of your experience to the job you are applying for. Even if you are not replying to an advertisement, you should give the potential employer some idea of what you are looking for, while also bearing in mind the type of employment they might have available. Describe what you did in each post succinctly, noting any special achievements. Make sure that you bring out the salient points in each job in a way that shows their relevance to the post you are applying for. Without lying, you can give prominence to the parts of the job that are now most important to your application.

Use short sentences and be bold – if you don't sing your praises nobody else will! You must say what you are capable of in a confident manner (without being too immodest). Give details of the skills you have; list what you *can* do and the achievements which can be credited to you. Do not simply say what you were better than others at, as the employer is unlikely to have any information on the others you are comparing yourself with.

Similarly, make sure that you don't become 'wordy', describing your talents in terms of what somebody else thinks. It can be offputting to read, *Mr Jones, my boss, said that I was always efficient in getting work done on time and that it was always right first time.* Note the difference if this was described as, *My work was consistently accurate and my efficiency valued.*

You may find it quite difficult to describe a whole job in a few sentences and this will take some thought, especially if you have specific achievements which need to be mentioned. The description should give a fair summary of your main duties and achievements. It does take time, so make sure that you don't skimp on this. Remember that your CV is the passport to the interview.

Try out different ideas on colleagues if possible, or on others in the field in which you are seeking work, to make sure that the information is clear and unambiguous. Avoid jargon phrases unless you are *absolutely certain* that the reader will understand them. You cannot know who will read your application first, particularly with a speculative attempt, and do not want your hard work discarded because somebody did not know the relevance of your experience.

You can save space by avoiding duplication if you have had several jobs where the duties were roughly similar. Give information about the employer and simply note *duties similar to those undertaken at. . . .* Make sure that this technique is only used when you have already described those duties, rather than making the reader check information further down the page. Make sure that the description relating to the employer is included in each section, however, rather than listing the names of the employers in one section and then muddling all the information together into a piece of lengthy prose below. Each employment entry should be clearly separated and should give the month as well as the year. See the example below.

Mansfield Taylors Ltd April 1990 – January 1995	Senior buyer

(Brief description of job)

K.L.B. Outfitters Ltd October 1986 – April 1990	Buyer

(Brief description of job)

It is unnecessary to give the addresses of your past employers but you should give the reader some idea of the kind of business that they were in if the employer is not well known. For instance if you simply quote,

J.M. Saunders and Sons   Finance assistant
July 1991 – September 1995

the reader will have no idea whether you were employed by a builders' merchant or a retail outlet, etc., and will have no idea how big the company was. This means that he/she will be unable to get a realistic grasp of the kind of work you have been doing, even if this is described in general terms below. All this needs is the addition of the words *local builders' merchants* for this to become clear.

In some cases a description of the work may be needed in slightly more depth if the tasks are not apparent from the job title. For example, 'Administrative Assistant' can cover a multitude of functions and may be very specific to one area of work, particularly in local government, etc.

If you have worked in a large organisation with a grading system, you will not need to include the grade of your post unless this is relevant and will be understood by the organisation you are applying to. If, however, you are applying to transfer from one area of local government to another, or within the national health system, etc., this information may be very useful to the prospective employer. If it is likely to be irrelevant or not understood, avoid mentioning it.

Make sure that any gaps in your employment are explained, as employers like to have a complete picture of what you have done. If you have been abroad travelling, etc., you need only put in the dates and give very brief details, for example, *travelled throughout South America for six months*. If you have undertaken any casual work during this time, this can be mentioned briefly if it is relevant. For other gaps, use your discretion (*see* later notes on sickness and prison).

Personal interests, hobbies and pastimes

Watch the weighting of this section as it should not take over from the rest of the CV! Although the employer will probably want a few details of your interests so that he/she can get an idea of what kind of person you are, it is the experience and qualifications section which are most important. (Note that an exception is made for school/college leavers as outside interests may be used to show an aptitude for certain types of employment.)

Try to balance your interests so that they show a mix of active and passive occupations. If your jobs have been mainly sedentary, you might wish to give more emphasis to your active hobbies, just to show that you are not always sitting down! Similarly, if your job involves lots of rushing around, a few passive interests can be included, to show the employer that you can relax and are not a candidate for a nervous breakdown!

Give an indication of the level of your interest and some idea of whether these show skills or just enthusiasm, for example, if you quote 'football' or 'dance' say whether you take part in this or just watch. Avoid references to your bronze medal in ballroom dancing, etc, unless this is relevant! If you are including references to sports, note that the employer may be looking for indications of whether you prefer team games or those where you compete as an individual. This too, can be used as a balance for other aspects of your life and experience.

Adding any information on any charitable work you undertake can be useful, showing you to be socially responsible and 'a nice person' as well as being used as another indicator of specific skills. However, it is advisable to omit details of your politics and religion, (in fact anything particularly controversial) unless you are making an application to an organisation which openly supports it. One final point to bear in mind is, though many of us spend time doing it, watching television is not considered an acceptable hobby to include!

Other details to include in your CV

Use you discretion about what else to include – the golden rule is that it must be relevant. Other details often included are:

- driving licence
- languages
- medical details
- salaries
- computer skills and/or packages used
- reasons for leaving
- references
- short courses undertaken
- publications
- career aims
- service experience

Driving licence

You should include the words *full clean driving licence* if you are answering an advertisement where company cars are given, or if you are required to be mobile. It may also be useful to add *own car* if you are prepared to use this for work. (If you have no driving licence, leave it out. If you have endorsements, you must use your discretion.)

Languages

If languages are likely to be required or you are applying to an organisation which has a foreign parent company, etc., this can be included. Give an indication of your proficiency and fluence. Note that rusty school French is usually not acceptable, leave it out! Naturally if you are a translator, this should not come under a separate section at the end, but can be included at the beginning if the languages are not apparent from a quick glance at the employment details.

Medical details

Unless you have a medical problem which the employer needs to know about, leave this out. They will assume that you are in good health unless you state otherwise. If however, you have had gaps in your employment or education due to sickness, recurring illness, etc., you would be wise to say to what extent you are still affected by this. If you are completely 'clear' and no longer affected, say so. You may find it useful to add a note to the effect that you have had no time off work sick since then.

Similarly, if you have a disability which will affect your employment you should mention it. Because prejudices still abound against people with disabilities, you will need to emphasise even more strongly what you are capable of, rather than focusing on what you can't do (or giving the reader a chance to do that), as first impressions stick.

Salary details

It is usually unnecessary to include details of your salary on your CV. If you are earning more than most of your peers in the same industry this may be worth mentioning in your covering letter, particularly if you will not accept any drop in salary. Salaries do vary very widely between organisations and stating your earnings can sometimes give a false indication of what you are worth. For instance, although some sectors or companies may be known as low payers, the reader of your CV may not be aware of the extent of this. In addition, salaries paid several years ago are no longer relevant. Let the potential employer judge you on your merits and what you can do, rather than what somebody else has paid you.

Computer skills

Computer skills are increasingly relevant and details of the kinds of software packages you have used are often helpful. Group these so that wordprocessing packages are together, as are database packages and spreadsheets, etc. If you are including programming, say to what level you are proficient and which languages or generations you are used to.

References

Many people send past (usually open) references with their CVs and applications. This is rarely relevant at this stage. As long as you make it clear that references can be provided at a later date there is no necessity to send them initially. Open references (those beginning *to whom it may concern*) are less useful anyway as they are invariably glowing (and you wouldn't send them if they weren't!). Many employers feel that the only really valid references are those which are obtained by them asking specific questions about your suitability for a particular job. Open references may of course be necessary if the employer is uncontactable, perhaps overseas or has gone out of business, etc., but keep these up your sleeve!

Short courses

It may be useful to include details of short courses you have attended if these are relevant. They can be valuable in showing that your knowledge is up-to-date. However, if you are not sure whether these will be received well, leave them out. (You do not want the reader of your CV to take one look and think that you will always be asking to disappear off on courses!)

Publications

Similarly, include details of publications only if they are relevant. Academics by convention include them all, but if the list seems endless, your entry could merely give one or two important examples and then say that you have written several other publications on this topic. If several topics are covered, they can be grouped together. Note that you may show publications as evidence of good written, communication skills.

Career aims

Some people include details of their career aims in their CV, particularly if they have changed areas of work, to show what they are interested in. This is only really useful if you are sending out many speculative letters to prospective employers, otherwise it can be easily noted in the covering letter.

Service experience

Again, the key word is relevance. If you have had a long and distinguished service career, you may wish to add details of this. In general, this can be included in the general employment history section rather than isolating it from other experience.

The overall effect of your CV

Your CV should be tidy and neat, with nothing crossed out and no smudges. Try to send an original and make absolutely sure that there will be no black photocopier lines along the edge. This is especially important if attention to detail and presentation will be important factors in the job you hope to get.

The CV should be in black ink so that it can be easily photocopied by the employer – a point to remember if you are having yours printed rather than just typed. (Again, use discretion on print versus type, and remember that printed versions are more expensive to update.) A4 format on white paper is often useful for the employer to copy and to fit into their files! Avoid highly-coloured paper which glares under fluorescent lights!

As mentioned earlier, pay special attention to spelling and grammar. If in doubt, look it up or use another word or phrase.

Try to match the style as much as possible to what you know of the organisation. Think about the image that you are portraying, for example, would a banking company really want to know all about your artistic skills? They are more likely to look for a CV where the stereotypes match, perhaps for a more staid and less artistic and volatile individual! If you are applying for a job where creativity is required, try to use your imagination on the CV without losing too much of the traditional format. But don't go mad!

6. Fine tuning your CV

Once you have the basic information on your CV, you will need to tune it finely to fit your own circumstances. In this chapter, special circumstances are dealt with along with pointers on how to beat the 'opposition'. These ideas are not exhaustive and you should aim to put in the required details in your own words.

School college leavers

This section applies to anyone without formal employment experience, where the work section of the CV will be missing. This means that your CV can be even more brief than for others; one side of A4 may be sufficient.

Note the points made earlier on grades and remember to be consistent in either putting in all of these or omitting them entirely. If you think that the employer will not understand what your qualifications mean, or are equivalent to, make sure that you put in a short explanation. Don't put in information that may be superseded. For instance, if you took typewriting exams for 30, 40 and 50 words per minute on the same day, you only need to mention the latter, provided that you passed it!

If you have any work experience which you gained either at school as part of the work-experience programme or which you undertook during vacations, mention it if it is relevant. If you had a three-week holiday job digging ditches or grapepicking, mention it only if it is relevant, not if you are applying for a job in a building society where it doesn't count. Any office-bound experience is worth mentioning if you are going to work in an office later as it shows that you were able to fit into an office environment. In fact, any general office experience is always valuable, whatever kind of office you are going to. If you do not have any qualifications and you have held a temporary job for, say, the whole of the vacation, you should put it in to show that you are able to 'stick at' working.

Employers are always looking for any evidence that you will stay in the job. Recruiting people is expensive and without any previous work experience, they will need to be convinced that you will stay in the job and not get fed up and leave, or constantly take days off sick. Staying power is important. Try to show that you have some pastimes which you have maintained an interest in to demonstrate your consistency. Also, show by everything that you say that you are keen and willing to work hard.

Be specific about the work experience that you have undertaken and what time periods that covered. If you can show that you settled into this well, and developed so that you were able to progress to accepting more advanced work than you undertook at first, this will be valuable. Any skills which you gained should be itemised.

Link your hobbies and personal qualities with the kind of work you want. If you are secretary to a local youth group, this will help you to demonstrate your organisational skills. If you have been the treasurer of a local club, your numeracy will be evident, etc. However, be careful about mentioning your involvement in student politics. Some employers still see universities as hotbeds of communism or may be worried that you are idealistic rather than realistic. If the circumstances feel right, you can always elaborate on these aspects at an interview when you can see what reaction you are receiving.

Unemployment and redundancy

If you have never been employed, see the section above. Give some indication of something you have been doing since you left full-time education. This may cover 'temping' in various jobs or part-time work, or if you have simply been trying to find a job, say so. Try to show that you have been using your time effectively, either by learning new skills or by systematic applications for posts. Be ready to explain why you think that you were unable to get a job elsewhere at the interview if you have been unemployed for a long period. Recruiters will be impressed by a frank and honest self-appraisal, as long as you can emphasise your strengths rather than your weaknesses.

If you have undertaken any freelance work, list this, perhaps calling it consultancy if the type of work merits it. Note, however, that employers will not be fooled if you say you have undertaken consultancy assignments which cannot be substantiated. If you have undertaken real assignments, list the type of work that you undertook for each company, and give the names and addresses of the organisations. This demonstrates that other employers are satisfied with your work and that you were able to gain worthwhile contracts. If you have undertaken a string of odd jobs, list these as various short-term contracts and again, give an idea of what kind of people/organisations you were working for.

However unfair it may seem and however much you need to express your dissatisfaction with being unemployed, your prospective employer will want to take on a cheerful worker. Make sure that you do not write your application when you are depressed as the words you use may well give you away and make you sound unconfident or overly negative.

If your last employer went bankrupt, you must divert any suspicion that it had anything to do with you or your work, particularly it you were employed on the financial side.

Never run down your last employer, or the reader of your CV may think that in time you will do that to them. Your aim is to show a responsible attitude without bitterness (whatever you actually feel!) and you must also avoid sounding *desperate* for work. Your job now is to convince the reader that you will be a loyal worker and a useful, productive member of the team.

Note that you will probably be unable to move into a higher-level post than you left. It is invariably easier to gain promotion *within* an organisation than moving between companies, and it is even more difficult to move up from your last level when you are not currently in a job. You may have to settle for something beneath your ability and then progress from there. Remember too, that you have points in your favour, including your ability to start immediately.

After your own business has failed

Similar in many ways to the above category, many employers are suspicious if they think that someone who wanted to work for themselves (and perhaps therefore does not want to be employed in the normal way) has not managed to achieve this. Frustrated entrepreneurs are not always in demand! The failure of your business may throw doubts on your motivation, your ability to handle money, your ability to convince other people (selling your services or products) and judge markets, and your staying power.

You will need to show clearly that these things are not accurate or true and that there were very good reasons for your return to the labour market (expressed briefly). Be succinct in your descriptions and give definite dates, particularly the end-point of your business. Again, any evidence of your main or other work will be useful.

Career breaks

If you have been away from the working environment raising a family, taking a sabbatical or extended travelling, your main difficulty may be convincing the employer that you are committed to being employed again. In addition, you may have to compete with people who have up-to-date experience and skills. Try to utilise the experiences you have gained. Once you have analysed these, you may well find that they have relevance to the employer in the same way that school leavers can demonstrate the relevance of their hobbies. Voluntary work undertaken may be useful for this.

If you have been raising a family you may need to satisfy an employer that you have good childcare arrangements and will not always be taking time off work if the children are ill. This may sound patronising and unnecessary, but you have to convince the recruiter that you are a worthwhile investment and would make a reliable employee. The same applies if you have been looking after elderly relatives and/or dependants. You may also have to prove that you are a stable individual and not in great distress (that you are in fact able to work effectively) if the relative(s) have died or been ill.

If you have worked abroad, you may be able to show that your work was similar and comparable to anything you would have undertaken here. In addition, any extra proficiency in languages may be useful as would an understanding of international commerce, etc. Make sure that any references and testimonials you provide are translated into English and witnessed as authentic.

If your career break has been due to imprisonment, you do not necessarily have to declare this. After certain periods, some convictions are deemed 'spent' and do not have to be declared. Although it is illegal for employers to discriminate on the grounds of spent convictions, it is difficult to prove.

If you decide not to put this on your CV, you must be prepared for questions about the gap in your employment at the interview. If you decide to include minimal details, you will necessarily have to limit yourself to attempting to find employment where the offence is not relevant. For instance, a conviction for theft may make a post in finance very difficult to attain so you would have to look for something unconnected.

In addition, there are various laws covering the employment of adults working with children which prohibit the employment of individuals with certain convictions. It will probably be helpful for you to obtain further advice on this if you wish to take up this sort of employment and you have a conviction.

Women

Despite the fact that women make up half the working population and you may not think that a special section is necessary, there are special points to be considered.

Although legislation is on their side, women often have difficulty in convincing employers of their loyalty; that they will not leave to have children or move to another part of the country because their partner has been moved. You may also want to forestall any thoughts that you would be unable to undertake necessary overtime. Tackle these points together with the childcare issue directly so that you can persuade the recruiter that this does not apply to you (or at least that they would gain long, loyal service from you first).

A few employers hold the opinion that women do not make good bosses. If you would have responsibility for other staff and you suspect that the employer may hold this view, give examples of the successful management of others if possible. (Then consider whether you really want to work for such a company!)

Ageism

Although there have been various (unsuccessful) efforts to outlaw this, many people still feel that advertisers are ageist and that they consider potential applicants 'over the hill' after forty. Some advertisers specify an age range but this is rarely an absolute rule (except for graduate-trainee schemes, etc.). Use your discretion, if you are close to the range, apply. If not, you may wish to telephone the organisation to ask whether there would be any flexibility within this.

You may wish to omit your date of birth from your CV, although the experience you quote and qualification dates will give an indication of your age. It may be more effective to stress the positive points of what you can do and add any phrases which make this sound dynamic or energetic. This can be done by association too, for example, if you can describe your current employer as a young company or fast-moving and dynamic. Your hobbies, if active, can be used to reinforce this, but you will have to be careful not to labour the point or paradoxically, the recruiter may think that you have had problems before because of your age and reject your application.

Dual employment

If you have had more than one job at once, state which was full-time (if applicable) and which were part-time. Show which you considered to be the 'major' employment. Make sure that the dates are clear and that this does not get muddled with any more conventional employment details.

If you have undertaken part-time paid work, give an indication of the level of your commitment to this. For instance, many senior managers also lecture and would show the number of hours per week that this entailed. If this kind of activity is to continue, ensure that it is obvious that this does not interfere with your 'main' employment. Remember that employers are ideally looking for someone who will prove committed to their company and not someone whose loyalties are divided.

Special points for specific employment

There may be other items that you will need to put in
which are particular to your kind of employment. For
instance, sales professionals would be likely to include
details of their sales targets met and superseded and
possibly the commissions they earned. Computer staff
may need to put in details relating to the hardware/
software and may use jargon which would not be
acceptable in other industries.

Secretaries and others whose titles may be
misinterpreted should give *precise* details of their level
of work, so that the potential employer can see
whether that job would be described as secretary, PA
or clerk/typist in their own organisation.

There is often a temptation for those involved in
anything artistic/creative to attach examples of their
work. Be guided by the industry norms on this and
note that, in the majority of cases, it is not wise to do
this. Additions to CVs are time-consuming for those
reading them, and therefore unpopular and portfolios
may not be returned. If you do attach examples that
you would like returned (and this is not advisable if
you can help it), submit a correctly-stamped, addressed
envelope for them.

Beating the opposition

Avoid clichés and try to ensure that the CV makes you
sound a nice person to have around (if you equal other
candidates on paper, the 'nice' person will win out!).
Your application (including your covering letter)
should be positive and enthusiastic. Don't itemise
weaknesses on the basis that your honesty demands it

or that it is only fair that they know. Itemise your strengths and dwell little on the bad points!

It will be useful to show, if you can, a logical progression throughout your career, with one area of work leading on to another. Don't waffle, but emphasise the strands which pervade your experience. This can be done by adding an extra paragraph at the beginning of the work history section, showing a summary of your experience. Show that you are self-aware, that you know what you are good at and what you want. The latter must of course be realistic and relevant to the organisation you are applying to.

Finally, each CV needs to have 'something special'; that ingredient which sets it apart from the others. You must develop this, perhaps by the use of your sense of humour, or by the insertion of unusual facts if that is applicable. You will have to work on this and develop your own speciality.

7. Application forms and the accompanying letter

Most of the points relating to application forms and covering letters are similar to those given in other chapters. However, there are some specific points which should be made.

Application forms

If you have already sent a letter and CV, you may be irritated to receive a request to complete an application form. Organisations use these, however, so that they can collect information about the applicants in a similar format (which makes it easier for them to compare people) and all the important details are covered. If you feel that the application form does not do you justice, you can add extra information or another copy of your CV to it.

When you receive the application form, photocopy it so that you can fill in a draft form before completing the original. This means that if you run out of space in one area you can change the wording or the size of your writing so that the final version fits into the right space. It also gives you a chance to see what the information looks like on the page and the opportunity to correct errors.

Read the accompanying company literature before you complete the application form. This may include a job description, hierarchy chart and possibly an annual report and details of the organisation. This will help you gear your answers to the job (see notes on angling your experience in previous chapters).

You should answer all the questions on the form and type or write clearly in black ink (as the form may be photocopied). If your writing is difficult to read, use capitals. Note that application forms are usually labelled 'confidential' so you should not be reticent about important details.

Note that you may be asked to fill in an application form at an interview (often as a formality), so that the interviewers have a note of the important details. It is a good idea to take a CV with you to an interview so that you can check dates, etc., that you might not otherwise remember. Few employers are impressed if the dates and details on two different forms are inconsistent.

Sections on the application form usually cover:

- personal details
- health
- education and qualifications
- work experience
- reasons for leaving
- leisure interests
- why you want the job
- a blank space for you to add any other relevant information

Personal details may be covered in more depth than you would include on a CV. For instance, some employers ask for details of your parents' birthplaces and nationality as well as your own. In some cases health questions appear on the main application form, asking about your general health and any serious illnesses/operations, or time off work at your last employment. In other cases, a separate health questionnaire may be included.

On the sections for education, qualifications and work experience, make sure that you complete the information in the order requested. For leisure interests follow the same advice given in the chapter on CVs.

Reasons for leaving

Most application forms ask for information on this. Remember that you will have to justify your reasons at an interview. It is not enough to say that you left one position to take up an offer at a new company. The reader will want to know why you were looking for other work.

Promotion is always acceptable, but beware of stating *personal reasons* or worse still *personality clash*. These always raise suspicions and the reader will think that you are unable to get on with people. No matter how many people your awful boss drove out, they can only see that you had a problem! Never criticise your employer and avoid any references that may show you in a bad light. For example, *overwork* can be taken to mean that you have no capacity for work, *boredom* may show that you were unable to find things to do on your own initiative. However unjustified this may seem, recruiters will want to ensure that you do not fall into these categories. It is not enough to think that you can explain at an interview as you may not get one if there are other good applications without any phrases which worry the recruiter.

If you left for more money, try to link this with more responsibility and/or challenge. Relocation of the organisation is an acceptable reason for leaving provided that you are not applying to an organisation which requires mobility, or possible relocation itself. Redundancy is also acceptable (a change from former days when it was sometimes a cover for being sacked). If you were sacked, do not lie but try to find a way of leaving explanations to the interview. You might perhaps say that there was not sufficient match between your aspirations and the job, or another such vague phrase. *Think* about what you will put here though, and use your discretion. *To be explained at interview* leaves readers curious or suspicious!

You will have to provide well-thought-out reasons for leaving if you have changed jobs frequently in an industry where this is unusual. Conversely, if the industry is fast moving, you may need to give some reasons why you chose to stay so long. Try to think about the phrases you use for this and ask the advice of others to make sure that a cynical interpretation would not be totally damning. Ask people who are not involved or who will not automatically see 'your side', because you are looking for impartial advice and help.

The 'blank space'

This section, often entitled *any other relevant details*, gives you the space to cover reasons why you want the job, any extra skills which have not been mentioned elsewhere in the application and further, relevant information you wish to add. You may be given an indication that extra sheets can be attached if you wish. Use the allotted space but do not add reams of extra paper! Remember that the reader is only human and may be faced with a huge pile of applications, so you do not want yours to be discarded because it is too long, however fascinating you think it will be for them!

Areas in the questionnaire such as this are designed to make you *think*. You should analyse what they are looking for (go back to the advertisement and job description) and summarise your relevant experience. Don't forget to include items not mentioned before; voluntary work, etc. But *don't waffle*, ensure that your comments are specific and relevant to the application.

Make sure that you give reasons as to what you can contribute to the company within the job and give brief details of *how* you can contribute, rather than just *why* you want it. You need to demonstrate not just what *you* want, but what *they* will gain.

Other items which sometimes appear on application forms are:

- salary information
- previous applications to that company
- referees
- whether you know anyone else who works for the organisation
- where you saw the advertisement
- details of driving licence
- language proficiency
- notice periods
- possible start dates
- dates on which you would be unable to attend an interview
- membership of professional bodies and/or trade unions
- details of previous convictions with dates

Salary information

This can include details of your current and past salaries as well as the salary and other benefits you are seeking. You should put down a figure if the form requests it. Remember that your current salary may be checked later in a reference but that the employer may use this information to shape the offer to you if there is no set grading and salary structure (they may not increase far above your existing salary even if they have more money budgeted for your post).

References

You will usually be asked to give the names, addresses and titles of two referees and may be asked whether these can be approached immediately. If your current employer does not know about the application, make sure that you state this clearly so that they will not be contacted without your prior agreement.

If you do not have a current employer, you should use your last employer if applicable. Employers invariably prefer this. For school leavers use academic references, rather than putting down names of individuals who have known you and can give personal references. Personal references are less helpful as the employer wants to know what you will be capable of in the job. In addition, personal references are much more likely to be glowing, rather than objective and unbiased!

The signed declaration

Use common sense on the other information required.

You should note particularly that the information must be true. Usually you have to sign a declaration to this effect and if the information is found to be false you could be dismissed after starting in the job.

Accompanying letters

You will need to send a covering letter with a CV or an application form. This should be brief, giving just the salient points. The main information will be in either the CV or the form, so your letter serves just as a guide to where to look for the most important points (important for this post, that is). It should give a summary of these, rather than just repeat chunks from your CV or application form.

Brush up on your basic letterwriting skills. (*See also* Chapter 4 on speculative letters.) Note the conventions regarding 'Dear Sir' and 'Yours faithfully', etc. If you are not sure, find a good book on the subject or ask someone whose knowledge you trust. If you are replying to an advertisement, use the same title. For example, if the requirement is to write to Mr John Smith, make sure that you address the letter to *Mr Smith* and not *Dear John*. Check your spelling and grammar and ensure that any advertisement reference is quoted clearly.

Your letter should be neat and well spaced, on good A4 paper, preferably plain rather than with floral designs, etc. The latter makes it look as if you are not taking the job seriously and your letter must look businesslike. In most cases, it is not important whether the letter is typed or handwritten provided that it is clear and legible. If you are a typist, however, but handwrite your letter, the reader may wonder why!

Use short sentences and avoid clichés or hackneyed phrases. Also phrases such as, *I have initiative . . .* or *I can communicate effectively at all levels . . .*, waste space. They cannot be proved directly. Use examples instead, to demonstrate these points.

The covering letter is particularly important with speculative applications as an unaccompanied CV will not tell the reader anything about what you are looking for and why you are interested in their organisation. If you can find out the name of the person who would deal with vacancies, address your letter directly to them. Avoid phrases such as, *You will not know me, but . . .* as they know that! Try to make your letter positive and enthusiastic, a memorable letter may be remembered if a vacancy arises later. Be careful not to overdo this though!

Unsolicited letters should not be much longer than other accompanying letters; perhaps four or five short paragraphs. You should cover why you want the job, your interest in the company, what you have done in the past and any other relevant information, such as when you are moving to their area and therefore available for interview. In any letter, unsolicited or accompanying an advertised application, let the company know the dates you will be unavailable for interview, due to holidays, etc.

Take it easy

Do not pressurise the potential employer or *assume* that he/she has time to meet you to discuss your application, if there is not a post available then. Remember that employers receive many approaches similar to your own. If you choose to telephone a prospective employer after writing such a letter, again, do not pressurise him/her into interviewing you. Even if they give in and have a job vacant, you may not get the job if you seem too pushy!

If you are writing to consultants who are screening applicants for a specific post for a company, or you are writing to them on a speculative basis, give them extra information such as your preferred location and the names of any large organisations which you would not want to work for. Even where they are seeking specific applicants, you may be asked whether you wish to be added to their database of job seekers.

8. Preparing for the interview

Well done! You have been invited to the interview and will therefore have beaten a lot of the competition already.

Interviews should not be frightening experiences if you are well prepared. This chapter covers the basic preparation which includes practising your answers for the interview. You can do this with a tape recorder, or just thinking through the questions and answers, but the better way is to 'role-play' the interview so that you can ask your 'interviewer' to surprise you with questions you may not expect, to see how you respond.

It is a good idea to understand what the interviewer is trying to achieve. Most libraries have a number of books on this and if you read one or two it will give you a good idea of the possible format and the type of questions that could be asked and why.

On invitation to the interview

Once you have received the invitation to the interview, you will need to make doubly sure that you understand what the job is all about. Look back at the advertisement and read between the lines. Find out everything that you can about the organisation. If they have not sent you any details such as a job description, annual report, company literature, ask for these. Find out anything else that you can about the organisation. Use your local library to find out more, from Extel cards, *The Kompass Directory*, *The Times 1000*, *Who*

Owns Whom, Dun & Bradstreet reports, etc. If the organisation is a big local employer, the local newspaper may have other details.

Use the information you have gained to give you a clearer picture of the organisation. It is useful if you can remember some of this in case you are asked what you know about the company, but don't learn chunks of information about the turnover and subsidiary companies, parrot-fashion!

Reply to the invitation confirming that you will attend on the appointed time and date. If you are unable to attend on the date they have suggested, telephone the organisation and explain this, pointing out that you are still interested in the post. In most cases, unless the interview dates have already been specified in the covering information, the times and dates can be re-arranged if necessary.

Check whether the organisation pays expenses if you need this. Large private companies and public organisations will usually pay these, at least for school leavers. There is a tendency for expenses not to be paid for more senior grades, as individuals are often expected to have the finances to pay for themselves.

If you decide that you do not want the job, or have accepted another, always telephone the organisation to inform them that you will not be attending.

Vital information about the interview

Ensure that you understand clearly the exact date, time and place of the interview. If you know what to expect it will help you to feel more confident. Ask who will interview you and how long they expect this to last. There are few things worse than being interviewed knowing that your boss expected you back at the office an hour ago, so give yourself plenty of leeway! You should also be told if there are any tests involved.

Make sure that you know how to get to the appointed venue. If you are unsure ask the interviewer for exact directions well in advance. (This will not be frowned upon, interviewers expect it and would much prefer their candidates to ask.) Try the journey beforehand if possible, so that you know how long it will take and **never be late**. Punctuality is more important at the interview than at almost any other time.

Find out who will be interviewing you, the individuals' names and their job titles. You may have to see more than one person, either in a panel interview where more than one person asks questions or sequentially, where you will meet one person who will then hand you over to be interviewed by somebody else.

Just before the interview

A day or so before the interview, and then again just before, you should refresh your memory by reviewing the information about the company, the advertisement and your application. If you have applied for a number of jobs, you may not find it easy to remember what you said to each prospective employer. Run through the possible interview questions in your mind, checking that you know what you will say in answer (the essence of your response rather than parrot-fashion recitals). If you are very nervous, try to burn off some of the nervous energy beforehand by walking around a bit. (If you run you'll probably end up feeling sick and/or sticky!) Breathe deeply to help calm yourself.

Your appearance is important. If you can walk past the organisation on a day before the interview as people are leaving, you will get an idea of the culture of the place and some guide as to the clothing and style, etc. Wear something slightly smarter than the people you saw as most people expect you to 'dress up' a little for the interview.

Avoid extremes in your appearance and wear something that you feel comfortable in. This does not mean, however, that you should turn up in jeans. Men should wear a suit and women, a suit, smart dress, or skirt and blouse/jacket. Make sure that your shoes are clean (no sandals as they are too casual) and that your appearance does not seem cluttered. Avoid jangling jewellery and very bright colours (your dress should be relatively conservative). Exceptions to these rules will be found in organisations such as the fashion and design industries, so find out what is the norm in your case.

It is wise to avoid having an 'interview suit' particularly if you have been trying to get a job for a while. This can then become associated with feeling uncomfortable and 'failing' at the interview. Ideally, you should have a choice of clothes so that you can decide what is most appropriate for the job and organisation. Avoid anything too tight which will show the perspiration as you get nervous!

You should arrive for the interview freshly washed, with clean fingernails and no overpowering smells. That means no alcohol, garlic or tobacco, just before the interview. Take care not to wear strong perfume or aftershave, in some cases this can actually have an adverse effect on the interviewer!

Waiting

Whilst you are waiting for the interview you may see notice boards in the building. Look at these to see what is on them as this gives another indication of the culture. Some notice boards are all work and rules, others full of flat-share requests and details of social activities!

If you are kept waiting a long time, ask the receptionist or secretary how much longer you will be delayed (politely!). Whilst even the best schedules can drift a little, you should not be kept waiting for much more than half an hour. If it is impossible for you to stay longer, explain this politely and ask to make another appointment.

Do not attempt to involve the secretary or receptionist (or anybody else around) in idle chat as you wait. Although this may help your nerves, it will stop them working and may go against you later. (Some interviewers ask the other people who have met the candidates for their opinions of them, particularly if it is difficult to decide between two of them.) Most people will exchange pleasantries, but don't expect lengthy conversations.

Practice role play

This is vital. In the real interview you only get one chance to give the right answer, whereas if you have practised you are less likely to 'dry up' and not know what to say, or drone on endlessly as you cannot put the information succinctly.

Use the information in the next chapter to help you work out the questions you are likely to be asked and practise the answers out loud, so that you convey the information you want to in the right tone. Practising with a friend (providing they are honest) will help you to gauge whether you sound confident and knowledgeable about what you are talking about. Interview nervousness can otherwise produce apologists or boasters as the individual hasn't quite hit the right pitch!

Do not memorise answers to questions so that they are word-perfect though, as this will sound false and artificial and don't use a script. You will probably not find that the question is put in quite the same way as you expected, so you could end up answering a different question as the 'key word' starts you off on your set answer. Practising means that you are clear in your mind about the information you wish to give, and if the question varies, you can adjust the answer accordingly.

Think positively both whilst you practise the role-play and just before you enter the interview room. You have beaten a lot of the opposition who were not invited to the interview and if you have worked out answers to the standard questions and the difficult ones, you should feel confident!

9. The interview

Confidence comes from knowing what to expect. In this chapter, we look at the interview format and the kind of questions you may be asked. Use your common sense and the information given in other chapters too, to help you find the 'right' answers for you. Be positive and honest about yourself and most importantly, **listen** to the questions. The interviewer will probably take notes throughout so that he/she can remember the salient points, but do not be put off by this.

Format of the interview

The usual format of the interview is:

- enter interview room, introductions and handshake
- general small talk to establish rapport
- initial questions, why you want the job, etc.
- questions on your experience
- interviewer gives you information about the job, company, terms and conditions, etc.
- your questions
- information on when you will hear the outcome
- leave interview room

Make sure that you enter the room confidently. Walk up to the chair and sit down, shaking hands firmly with the interviewer first if he/she initiates this. Walk slowly if you are nervous.

The interviewer will probably ask you whether you had problems finding the place and will make small talk to help you to relax before the interview itself begins. Some interviewers will ask you wide-ranging questions first, such as why you want the job, or will say, 'tell me about yourself'. Have a well-prepared summary, don't ramble! Your reasons for wanting the job should be 'respectable', so you should answer in terms of the job itself rather than saying, 'I want more money'. If asked to 'talk about yourself' initially keep to what you think you can offer in the job, then add a bit about your personal characteristics (such as reliability and sense of humour).

A good interviewer will ask you open questions rather than those requiring simply a yes or no answer. If you are faced with closed questions, try to add an example or qualifying sentence to these. Monosyllabic answers will not help to convince the interviewer. You may also be told at the beginning what kind of questions you will be asked, particularly in a panel interview situation where each member of the panel may ask you questions on a different subject.

Contra-indications

The interviewer will be on the lookout for contra-indications during the interview, that is, those give-away phrases that may show undesirable qualities. These can cover dishonesty, irresponsibility, possible insubordination, laziness, lack of motivation, lateness, lack of commitment, badmouthing the employer and disruptive elements.

The interviewer will probably ask you questions about subjects in blocks, covering your qualifications and education (unless these were completed a long time ago, or need no further explanation). It is likely that questions will also be asked on your work experience, ambition and motivation, personal interests, personality, health and background. Remember that the employer has to try to appoint somebody who will stay in the job for the required length of time. They don't want someone who will get bored and leave, who will be constantly taking time off sick or who will never put in a full day's work. Note that your likes and dislikes may reveal a lot about your motivation and basic character.

You may be asked to talk the interviewer through your CV or education and experience, or you may be asked specific questions. This means that you may have to remember all the important points without being prompted. Make sure that you can do this fluently, if possible showing a logical progression from one post to another. If you are asked specific questions, typical examples might be:

Qualifications

Why did you study x at school?
What grades did you achieve? Do you think you could have done better?
What was your dissertation on?
What training have you had since you left full-time education?
Are you willing to undertake further training? (day release, etc.)

You may also be asked to elaborate on any qualification that the interviewer is not familiar with. If you are a school/college leaver, it is likely that there will be more questions on this subject.

Experience

What does your present job involve?
Why do you want to leave?
What do you enjoy most/least about your job?
What do you find easiest/most difficult in your job?
What are your greatest achievements/failures?
Why did you choose this career?
Why did you move from x job to y?
Why were you made redundant?
Is this job a step down for you?
What kind of work are you looking for?
What other jobs have you applied for?
Can you give examples of your initiative/problem-solving ability?
Have you managed other staff?

Be enthusiastic about your job. Keep your answers fairly short and if necessary ask if the interviewer would like more detail. If this is the case you can then expand your answers further.

You will also be asked specific questions relating to the job which may test your knowledge and competence or may simply be 'can you spell?', 'are you numerate?', etc. You may also be asked about your working style so that the interviewer can get an idea of whether you prefer working alone or as part of a team. (Ideally show that you can do both, but reveal a preference for whatever situation this particular job requires.)

These questions may also cover such topics as supervisory experience and leadership skills and whether you can meet deadlines or work under pressure. You may be asked to give examples of the pressure you are used to and what you do to 'wind down' afterwards.

The interviewer may also be trying to find out whether you challenge decisions made or accept them passively. There is no one right answer for this, you will have to use the culture of the organisation as your guide. In some organisations, new ideas and healthy discussion about why things are done that way are welcomed, in others it is seen as a threat to the management.

Follow guidance given in other chapters on reasons for leaving, and make sure that these are relevant. For example, if there are no real promotion prospects in this job the interviewer may be worried if you say that you wanted more challenge and promotion as your reason for leaving the last two jobs.

Follow guidance given in other chapters for school leavers, people returning to work after absence or made redundant, etc. The same principles apply to the interview answers as to what is put on your CV.

Ambition and motivation

You may be asked questions on what you would like to be doing in five years time, how this job would fit into your career plan, or how long you would expect to stay in this job. Try not to answer with clichés such as 'I'd like to be in your job'. If you would, describe the type of work you are aiming for rather than suggesting that you would oust your interviewer! Base your answers to the ambition questions on what you have found out about the norms of the industry and keep them realistic. Your chances of being chairman with no previous experience is pretty slim.

Other questions you may be asked will probe your motivation:

What sort of people do you get on with best?
What sort of people do you find most difficult to get along with?
What would you do if you won the pools?
Which motivates you more, money or power?
Do you think you are a competitive person?

There are of course many variations on these questions, but if you are aware of why they are being asked you will find it easier to produce an appropriate answer. If you don't know what you want to do in the future, tell the interviewer that this job is your ambition for the moment and that if you were offered it you would rethink your future from there.

There are seldom any right answers to the money/ power questions, but think about which would be better suited to the job you have applied for. For instance, in sales, money may be the expected answer, particularly if you earn incentive bonuses! But, if you are required to motivate and/or persuade in this job power may be your preferred answer.

Interests and personality

What do you do in your spare time?
Tell me about your leisure interests
Which newspaper do you read?
Are you competitive?
What do you consider your greatest strengths/ weaknesses?
What makes you angry?

What personal qualities do you have which make you suitable for this job?

Again, there are many varieties of these questions. They are designed to give a truer picture of your character, sometimes with a view to deciding whether you would fit in with the rest of the team. This is where you might demonstrate your sense of humour and easy-to-work-with nature, but don't fall into the trap of talking animatedly about your hobbies when your job has been described in a monotone!

Health

If you have not already answered questions on an application form you may be asked how many days you had sick last year, about any health problems and how you cope with pressure, etc. If poor health was a reason for leaving somewhere in the past, show that this is no longer a problem.

Turning the questions around

If you are asked about something that you haven't done, rather than directly admitting no experience without saying anything further, try to show that you know what is involved or that this skill is demonstrated by other experiences you have. If you have analysed your skills before writing your CV, you will be aware of your transferable skills; that is, those which show abilities which can be transferred from one setting to another. For instance, stock control involves numeracy skills and minute taking is similar to report writing in that both require analysis and a precis.

Clichés to avoid

In most cases you should try to demonstrate the ability you wish to convince the interviewer of through examples, rather than simply trotting out hackneyed phrases. If you think you can rise to a challenge, demonstrate it by giving examples of when you have done this in the past.

Avoid 'I'm good with people' as it says little about what you can do. Are you good at listening, understanding, motivating, inspiring or negotiating? If you are just good at chatting, leave it out! Oral presentation must of course be seen by the interviewer to be convincing. It is no good saying that you are an effective communicator if the interview has reduced you to a stuttering jelly!

Other clichés to avoid include:

'*I have extensive experience in. . .*'
People who say that often haven't, if they have, it shows.

'*I don't mind what I do*' or '*I would be interested in any job here.*'
This looks as if you are totally clueless about what you want, and worse still, what you are good at.

'*Don't search any further. You have found the right person.*'
Well, would *you* fall for that pushiness?!

'*Have I convinced you? Will you offer me the job?*'
Don't put the interviewer on the spot, particularly if you know that he/she has other candidates to see.

'*I know the type of person you are looking for.*'
Never presume!

Successes and failures, strengths and weaknesses

You will need to talk about your strengths and successes in the interview, without boasting, because if you don't tell the interviewer nobody else will – interviewers are seldom clairvoyant! Don't show off though. It will be seen as boasting if you say that you are consistently better than others (except in sales, where you may be able to show the results) or if you continually use superlatives about yourself. You should say that you are good at something, rather than brilliant.

Try to minimise your failures or at least show a good reason why success was difficult. If you are asked about personal weaknesses, choose those that will be least damaging in the job you have applied for. A proofreader would be foolish to say that their weakness was lack of attention to detail, for instance! Poor handwriting can be used as an example by many, as it has little to do with performance of the main duties!

Don't volunteer your weaknesses if not asked – this is not dishonest if you tell the truth with other aspects. Everyone has weaknesses as your interviewer well knows. Don't apologise for yourself but give the impression that you are confident even if you don't feel it. Phrases such as 'I'm afraid' as well as 'I'm sorry' tacked on the beginning or end of sentences are a real give-away!

Note that even if you are asked about your notice period in the interview, this does not necessarily mean that you will be offered the job, sometimes this is a standard question. Do not relax, thinking 'I've got it!' and proceed to tell the interviewer all your bad points!

Awkward questions

Every now and then we are asked something that really stumps us! If this is to do with your knowledge of a subject area, you will have to be honest and admit that you do not know or cannot remember. You may then wish to ask the interviewer what the right answer is. If the question probes your personality, ask the interviewer for a moment to think about it before answering. Don't worry, this will not go against you.

If you can, reflect the question back to the interviewer or ask for clarification or further information, which will give you time to think. Sometimes this will give you a better idea of what is being asked, and in some cases the interviewer will prompt you or start to give the answer themselves! Good interviewers will be probing areas of possible weakness in which case you can expect to feel a little uncomfortable. Try not to be too put off and remember that this will be happening to all the other candidates too.

Whatever you do, do not argue with the interviewer. If you disagree with what is being suggested, say so calmly giving your reasons in as non-contentious a way as possible.

Your questions

Usually at the end of the interview, you will be given a chance to ask any questions you have (although this does not mean that you should not ask questions along the way if clarification is needed). Make sure that you have prepared these before you go. Use a checklist if you think that you will not remember them all and do not be afraid to produce this if it will help you.

If the interviewer has answered everything you were going to ask, tell them that and repeat the questions that you were going to ask so that they realise that you had thought about it. Don't manufacture extra questions for the sake of it, if you have none.

Make sure that your first questions are about the job itself or the organisation and keep the ones on terms and conditions until after you have asked others, or you will only appear to be interested in the money. All interviewers like to think that you will be coming for the job, not just the loot!

Ask any further questions about the job so that you get a clear idea of what you would be doing. You do not want to find that you are offered a job, but are not sure whether you want it or not because you have too little information. Make sure that you know who you would be reporting to and how your performance in the job will be assessed (especially if the organisation awards merit pay!).

If it has not already been covered, ask why the vacancy arose, and why the last person left (or if this is a new job, why it has been created). This may give you some insight into the problems of the organisation, particularly if the last incumbent did not stay long. Try to find out how long the last person stayed and how long you would be expected to stay. If the person has been promoted this may bode well for you, as long as they do not continue to stay and block your further progression. Find out what your promotion prospects would be.

It is not generally useful to ask how many people they are seeing. The statistics are unimportant, what matters is whether or not you are offered the job! You should have gone into an interview to do your best so the calibre of the competition will not make any difference to that.

Ask when you will find out whether or not you will be offered the job. (Note that in some cases, this may be whether or not you will be invited to a second interview.) This is a legitimate question as the interviewer is seldom in a position to make you an offer there and then. If you have already been offered another job but would prefer this, tell the interviewer politely but without putting pressure on them. Usually they will endeavour to get you a speedy answer so that you will not lose out. However, in some cases a speedy answer will still be a couple of weeks.

Whilst questions about the terms and conditions should not come first, you will need to know the basics. If these have not been explained, ask the questions that you need answers to. This will usually include salary, but may also be holidays, pension, etc., or working hours; particularly if you might need to vary these because of your personal circumstances. If you do not desperately need the information, omit questions on sickness benefit and notice periods in case the interviewer thinks that you are likely to be absent frequently or wish to leave soon.

If you would not accept a post on the stated salary, you should say so. However, this is not an opportunity to negotiate, which only occurs once you have been offered the post. Sometimes, if asked what the starting salary would be, interviewers will ask what you want, so be prepared for this before you go. Your answer must reflect what you think you are worth and how much you think the organisation values the post, but be guided by industry norms if possible. It is also useful to find out when the organisation would intend to take up references.

Body language

The tips given previously should help you to combat interview nerves, and help you to think in a positive way. Tell yourself that you are being interviewed because you are a good candidate.

Throughout the interview, your body language must fit what you are saying otherwise the interviewer will be confused, perhaps not believing what you have said. Most of us are unconsciously very good at reading the feelings of other people – think of a time when you asked if somebody was upset or angry and their 'no' did not convince you at all because of what you were seeing.

When you enter the room, put any belongings away from you (safely rather than just where someone bringing coffee will trip over them!) and don't slouch. (Refuse the coffee if your hands are liable to shake.) Walk into the room slowly to help you stay calm and compensate for your jumpiness. Your handshake should not be limp and your smile should not resemble an inane grin! Remember that first impressions stick. When you do your role play, practise this part too.

Don't be over-familiar with the interviewer. Call them by the name they have introduced themselves by, rather than necessarily calling them by their first names and acting as if you had known them all your life! Eye contact is important. Look at the interviewer as you talk to him/her. Looking down or away creates the impression that you are shy or shifty! Wait for the interviewer to ask the first question and respond to that. Remember that the first few questions are the 'warm up' and the questioner does not want chapter and verse on the intricacies of your journey!

Your speech should be clear and audible; don't put your hand across your mouth. Try to ensure that you sound enthusiastic rather than monotonous (this is where practising really helps). If you talk too much you will doubtless be revealing your weaknesses rather than your strengths! Other signs of nervousness you must watch for are a squeaky voice, talking too fast and blurting out answers or speaking too quietly.

If you find that the attention of your interviewer has wandered, take that as a warning and use a pause in your speech to regain their attention. Then stop talking about that subject as quickly as possible and let the interviewer guide you to another topic.

Your attitude to the interview should show that you take it seriously. Show respect for the interviewer (as he/she should for you), avoid sarcasm and never attempt to flirt or put the interviewer down.

10. Other methods of selection

In some circumstances, candidates are not selected on the basis of an interview alone. Towards the end of this chapter you are given some basic information on some of the tests you may encounter. If you are likely to have to undertake several of these, perhaps for different employers, try to gain some more information about them from the organisations and/or by reading more comprehensive books on this.

Interviews, too, can vary and in some cases panel or group interviews are used. Interviews with people you know can pose special problems.

Panel interviews

You may be questioned by a number of people during a panel interview and the number of questioners varies. Many organisations now interview with at least two people together as standard and this is often preferred by organisations with a commitment to equal opportunities. The aim of this is to eliminate bias (both interviewers see the same performance and therefore should reach the same conclusions and prejudices should be counterbalanced). It also saves time, as the interviewers see the candidates concurrently.

Often the panel will be chaired by one individual who will do the introductions and the rounding-up comments at the end. The interview is likely to be more formal than a one-to-one as there are more people to ask questions, which usually come in blocks;

four questions from one person followed by four from the next, etc. Punctuality is even more important here as the panels often run on a tight schedule.

The interview may be slightly longer than with only one interviewer as each asks predetermined questions concerning their area. Also the 'settling down' time is likely to be longer as you will have to try to establish rapport with several people at once. Think of the interviewers as you would a group of friends, directing your gaze by sweeping your eyes from one to another (not too fast) and ensuring that each of them can hear you. This way you should be able to make eye contact with each one. Answers should be addressed mainly to the person who asked the question but you should also turn to look at other members of the panel.

Ignore any signals between panel members which will usually be aimed at keeping themselves in order and to time, rather than any criticism of you.

Promotion interviews and interviews with people you know

Whether this is a promotion interview or not, you may be faced in the interview by someone you know. Do not assume that because of this it will naturally go your way. Interviewers have to be fair to outside candidates and other internal candidates too, so they often try to discount what they already know about you, as much as they can. It is, therefore, just as important that you stress all your good points and think through the possible questions just as you would in any other circumstances. It is a common complaint that internal or known candidates are too complacent, do not do their homework and, therefore, may fail to be offered the job. Make sure that you prepare doubly well.

Think of all the negative things that the interviewer might bring up (including things which may have been said at your last appraisal assessment, if applicable) and be ready to counter these politely. Don't parade your weaknesses because you assume that the interviewer knows them anyway, he/she may have forgotten about a past mistake unless you bring it up again.

If you have applied for a post which will give you promotion to a job where there are tasks that you have not done before, think about how you would perform these and what you would do to learn. For instance, if you are applying for a post which means that you would have responsibility for staff for the first time, think about how you would deal with them. If you have time, read a good book on supervision and management and ask the advice of others whose opinions you respect. You should also make sure that you can describe a theoretical strategy for dealing with problem employees. Think about these new tasks which you will be faced with and develop your answers accordingly.

In a promotion interview, you must show that you can understand and perform the duties of the new job and are not simply good at the things you are used to in your current job. You must show potential.

If you are worried that you will not be promoted because your employer does not want to lose you from the job that you are doing, you will have to ensure that you point out politely that you have reasonable ambitions and that you are looking for a more responsible opening. They have to realise that you might leave if you cannot obtain a justified promotion. Beware of making threats though, particularly if you are not sure whether or not you are qualified for the new post. You could point out in a humorous way that it would be easier to fill your old post than this one! Another point in your favour will be that you already know so much about the organisation which should mean a shorter training time.

Second interview

If you are invited to a second interview, you will be one of a small number of candidates. Usually, at this stage the employer will have decided that you are capable of doing the job. He/she now has to choose who will perform most effectively in the post and will fit in best with the organisation and the team.

Don't keep trying to convince the interviewer that you are capable of performing the functions, but rather show that you fit in with the organisation. You may face more probing questions on what you think the company is trying to achieve, your motivation, etc. It is important, prior to this second interview, that you go back to your original assessment of the organisation so that you can prepare possible answers to this.

There may also be particular skills in which you have strength that are important for the job. The second interview is another opportunity for you to sell yourself but this should be a low-key sell, without any pressure. Don't be too laid-back though, and remember to show that you are still interested in the job. In the second interview you must stress the *contribution* that you are able to make to the organisation rather than focusing on what you *want*.

Group selection

This is less common and tends to be used where the interpersonal and communication skills of the candidates need to be tested. In group selection processes, candidates may be interviewed together. This may be in competition for a job or may be just to test how dominant/passive you are in a group, where individuals have applied for different jobs in the organisation. Try to find a balance between blending with the wallpaper and standing out from everyone else. Interviewers tend to avoid those who seem extreme.

You may have to take part in a group discussion, which is likely to be on a current affairs topic or similar, where nobody is likely to have any particular specialist or prior knowledge. This is your opportunity to demonstrate clear, lucid arguments.

In the group exercise, do not act, as the assessors will see through this. In general they are highly trained to watch and analyse behaviour. Don't argue with the other group members or attempt to bully them. You should attempt to persuade people to your views gently and politely rather than stamping your mark loudly on the group.

Assessment centres and job-related tasks

Assessment centres are expensive to run and attendance usually lasts over a day or two. Naturally this means that they are used where the employer expects to keep staff for some time. They are also used where interpersonal and communication skills are important and where your private life may merge with your work life, for instance if you wish to become a pub manager, or have to entertain clients often.

Employers feel that this method of selection gives them a true picture of the individual. You cannot be on your best behaviour for that length of time or the tension will show! The potential employer finds out whether you are really suited to the post or not.

Assessment centre programmes are made up of a number of exercises, tasks and interviews. The tasks are related to the job, so that for instance if you have to do regular presentations in the job, this is likely to be one of the tasks at the assessment centre. There may be group exercises where the group have to find the answer to a problem or where a leaderless group has to discuss an issue; this tests your skills of analysis and persuasion. Alternatively you may be assigned roles within the group and be asked to solve a problem.

If you are involved in a group problem-solving exercise, keep your cool. You should maintain both your involvement and your calm! This can be quite difficult as other people will be trying to persuade you of things that you may not agree with and these sessions are often designed to make everyone sweat, particularly if you are competing against another group! Don't be resistant to acknowledging somebody else's good idea though.

You may also be asked to take part in timed pen-and-paper exercises, either multiple choice questions measuring your aptitudes or personality etc., or problem-solving, write-a-memo, type exercises.

There will inevitably be social occasions during the course of the assessment centre schedule, for example when you gather together to eat. All the normal rules of etiquette apply, so don't slurp the soup, eat with your mouth open, etc! Make sure that you do not overdo your intake of alcohol, if you drink any at all. If you begin with a gin and tonic, add more tonic only and pass on the gin. Too much alcohol can blunt your ability to take part effectively in later exercises or can make you reveal too much about all your weaknesses! Employers will want to assess what you are like with clients and do not wish to think that you will be drinking too much, however well you appear to handle it!

Psychological and aptitude tests

These may be part of an assessment centre programme or used together with a traditional interview, at the organisation and they usually have a time limit. Simple aptitude tests include typing tests, and others where the level of skill is measured against predetermined criteria. These test the actual behaviour.

Knowledge tests assess your recall of factual information and level of knowledge and sometimes an analysis of data (like an exam). If you have to complete intelligence tests, try to be as accurate and fast as possible, with the emphasis on the former.

Personality tests and personal-interest questionnaires and inventories give the employer some idea of your basic personality traits. Unless you know exactly what you are doing, these are difficult to fake. They are generally used in conjunction with interviews to show up any potential problems and it is your ability to do the job which is more important than your personality. However, employers may worry about some traits. For instance, airline pilots generally have low outcomes on personality criteria showing imagination and creativity

– who wants to fly with somebody who, when tired, thinks he's seeing pink elephants! This exaggerated example gives the clue to the fact that these tests usually only highlight unacceptable extremes and anything within normal boundaries will not be a problem. So relax, don't try to give especially clever answers and do your best!

Medical examinations

You should already have been informed if the organisation wishes you to undergo a medical examination. Sometimes these are included in the selection process although it is more common for this to be left until a job offer is to be made to you. Alternatively, you may be asked to have a check-up with your own doctor who will then pass the results to the organisation.

You are unlikely to be able to avoid this process, so if asked, give in gracefully and recognise that you are lucky to get a health check for free!

11. Review your application

Whether you have been invited to an interview or not, you should review your application. Keep a diary of your applications so that you can check easily to see the percentage where you are being invited for interview and the percentage of job offers.

When rejected before interview

If you were not invited to interview, and particularly in cases where this has happened several times (not including speculative letters), you should look back over your applications to see whether you are applying for posts at too high a level. There may of course be other reasons which will, in the end, just require your persistence. This may be the case if you are older than the average recruit in that job, or have fewer qualifications, etc. If you are not sure of the reasons, see if you can obtain any feedback on why you did not get further.

For this you may wish to telephone the organisation to ask them for their assessment but you should be very careful not to question their judgement, just ask for any pointers which they could give you which would help in the future. Do not under any circumstances put pressure on them, attempt to change their minds or argue that you were an ideal candidate.

Make a note of whatever you are told and use this information when preparing your next application. This feedback is valuable, the opinions of those recruiting should be respected as they can give you objective information. Note however, that they will probably give you the polite version of the outcome, as nobody likes to tell someone that they were a 'no hoper'! If the interviewer says that there were many well-qualified people, ask what the ideal qualifications and experience were. If they tell you what they were looking for and you think that you had got those attributes, do *not* say so, but recognise that you had not communicated this effectively. You must read between the lines and probe politely on anything you do not understand. Remember, though, that the person you are talking to may be busy and not have time to chat.

After the interview

You should attempt to write up the details of the interview immediately afterwards whilst this is still fresh in your memory. You may note certain questions that were asked which can remind you to prepare these again in the future. Make a special note of any particularly awkward questions or your particularly good answers to them! Note any questions which made you feel very uneasy as this will probably have shown. It is often said that interviewees think of all the clever answers after they have walked out of the interview room and into the street. Write them down, then and there, so that you can use them next time!

If you are not offered the post, ask for information on why not. Following up does take courage, but the feedback you can obtain will make it worth it and hopefully help you to obtain the offer of a post on your next attempt. The objective of getting feedback is to gain further information for the next occasion. Again, you may wish to telephone the organisation or write a short letter (you are more likely to obtain a response over the telephone though). As above, be sure that you give no hint of criticism and emphasise that you just want their help so that you can put in a better application/performance at interviews on future occasions. People are more likely to respond if you appeal to their vanity, flatter them a little. (Don't overdo it!) Say how much you would value their expertise and informed opinions.

If you are unable to get through to the interviewer on the telephone, do not leave messages requesting, or worse still demanding, that they call back. If you irritate the interviewer you are unlikely to gain his/her co-operation – dogged persistence here seldom pays off. If the interviewer is not willing to give you any further information you will have to accept this. Never be rude; the person is doing you a favour by giving you some feedback. Interviewers change jobs too, and if you are rude to them, you do not want to find them facing you at another interview for another company!

Grounds for complaint

However much you may feel you have been treated unfairly, do not write to the interviewer's senior, which will only damage you in the end, as they are practically certain to uphold the interviewer's decision. Also, provided that the new recruit can do the job, that is all that will concern the manager. If you believe that you have genuine grounds for grievance under the Race Relations Act or the Sex Discrimination Acts, etc., take this up with the relevant agency rather than battling directly with the organisation.

If you are telephoning the organisation, have a

notebook handy so that you can record the comments made, enabling you to remember them. If the interviewer says (without prompting from you) that it was a close decision and you were obviously capable of doing the job, you should believe this. The successful candidate may have been slightly better on one or two aspects and no doubt your worth will be recognised by other organisations in the future. In a number of cases, interviewers find that they are spoiled for choice and that a number of the candidates could do the job, they are therefore attempting to pick the best person.

As mentioned above, read between the lines and recognise the limits of what you will be told. If the interviewer did not trust you or did not have confidence that you could perform some of the functions efficiently, they will be unlikely to tell you. Listen for what is not said, having asked what they were looking for and what were important aspects in the job.

If the organisation did not appoint anyone from the interviews, try to find out what they were looking for in the candidates. Undoubtedly they will recognise that there has been a problem and will try to rectify this. Note that politeness will probably pay off. If you really were the second choice and the first choice candidate refuses the job, you may still get the offer. Obviously this is not a common occurence, but it does happen. Also, there may be a possibility of them keeping you on file in case another vacancy arises.

Even if you are offered the post feedback is always useful. Keep it in store for the next time you wish to make a career move. Recognise what they thought your strong points were and work out where you might have been weaker!

When you are offered the post

Once you have been offered the job, ensure that you have enough information on which to make a considered opinion. In some cases, you may know that it is exactly what you want. In others you may wish to explore other possibilities or just to think about it before you make a final decision.

If you find that you require more information, telephone the organisation to find this out or make a further appointment to see the person who interviewed you or your new boss, as appropriate. Never hand in your notice until you have received the offer of the post in writing.

12. Assessing the job offer

Usually you will be telephoned with a job offer and the confirmatory letter is sent later. Wait until you get the offer in writing before handing in your notice or attempting to negotiate on the salary. Don't leave any negotiations until after you have accepted the offer, or you have started the job, though, as before then is your main chance to make any changes you require.

Some letters offering employment are more detailed than others and give a multitude of facts that you will need to know. If there is any tentative arrangement which has been mentioned at the interview but is not written into your letter or contract, follow this up. This may include an agreement to honour holidays you have already booked, provide a company car after a certain length of time, or your promotion to a senior level after an agreed time period. Whatever the interviewer has said about 'something can be sorted out', if it is not down in writing it has not been sorted out! Remember that even if you trust the interviewer, he/she may leave before this happens and if nobody else in the organisation has any record of the agreement, it may not be honoured.

Whilst awaiting another offer

If you receive an offer for one post but would prefer to take another, you may be able to delay your acceptance of the first by a few days. It is only fair to telephone the organisation to let them know the position and give them an idea of when they can expect an answer. It is rare for you to be able to keep them waiting long though, naturally they need to fill the post and may be unable to keep the offer open for long.

Telephone the organisation which has the job you really want and find out how long things will take there. Explain politely that you have another offer but would prefer their job, without putting pressure on them. If you have already been interviewed, they may be able to let you have an answer fairly quickly. If not, you may have to make a decision about the first job before you hear from them. Use your discretion.

Information you need at the offer stage

There are a number of items of information that you will need when you receive the offer. A checklist of important information you may require includes:

- is the offer conditional? If so, on what?
- starting date
- starting salary
- date of salary progressions
- grade of the job
- exact location of the job
- probationary period
- induction training (may be residential or distant from your location)
- relocation assistance (if applicable) and repayment details
- details of other financial arrangements or fringe benefits such as commission, bonus schemes, pension, car allowance, share options, medical/life insurance, staff discounts, luncheon vouchers and social club membership

Conditions

Most offers of employment are conditional on receiving satisfactory references. They may also be conditional on a satisfactory medical check, the verification of your qualifications or your production of a valid work permit, etc. Make sure that you know any conditions and if you anticipate any problems, let the organisation know. Don't wait for them to find out.

For instance, if you are expecting a bad reference, tell the company. If you anticipate that this will be because your current employer does not want you to leave, say so. (Note that if you can ask to see any reference your present employer is about to submit, this may minimise the damage.) If your worry is based on something more serious, make sure that you provide the organisation with your version first! If you have a few medical problems, show the extent to which these might affect your work, or the time off that you will need to take. Work permits can often take a while to come through. If you need one, make sure that the organisation knows as they will have to provide details of your employment.

Make sure the date of starting work is correct and as you had agreed or expected. The employer should normally honour your notice period with your current employer (after all, they will expect you to work out your notice with them!).

Details of the offer

Make sure that the salary matches your expectations. If this is lower than you had expected, telephone the company and sort this out. They should send an amended offer letter if there has been a mistake. If the organisation has a grading structure, you should be given details of your grade, the structure and where your grade fits into the overall system.

If you have been promised a future increase in salary, perhaps after your probationary period has been satisfactorily completed, make sure that this has not been forgotten. If there is a standard progression system, you should be provided with details of it. If this does not happen automatically, ensure that you can see some reference to it either in your letter or the contract of employment.

Note that most posts have a probationary period – make sure that you know how long this will be and how you will be assessed. You may have a different notice period within the probationary term, which is a safeguard for you and the employer so that you can leave quickly if things do not work out.

You may also be required to attend an induction course for the company so that you gain an understanding of their various business functions. Sometimes these are held on the premises, but in other cases they are well away from the organisation, perhaps residential, so that you are not disturbed or called back by others in the office! Make sure that the organisation is aware if a residential course would cause you problems because of your personal circumstances.

You should be informed of the location of the post. Note that there may be references within the contract to your willingness to move with the company, known as mobility clauses. You may have to travel frequently but would be required to be at the main office once a week, etc. Make sure that your are willing to accept this.

If you have been offered relocation assistance, ensure that you are aware of the exact terms and that you know the system for paying this back if applicable. Note that these offers are very often attached to conditions which make the repayments punitive if you leave within three years or so. There may be other financial or fringe benefits that you have been offered. These can include everything from luncheon vouchers to share options. The details of any of these should be given to you – note that there may be qualifying periods for some of these.

There are a host of other details which may be included in your contract. These cover your notice period with the new company and the needs of the organisation which are specific to it. For instance you may have access to confidential information and have to sign a company secrets agreement, or the Official Secrets Act. There may be a specification for you to undertake further training. You may be required to hold membership of a particular recognised trade union. You may have a requirement not to have any other jobs whilst you are with the organisation (to stop outside part-time work or 'moonlighting'). In sales posts, you may have your 'patch' specified, that is the geographic area in which you can sell the company's goods or services. It is impossible to give an exhaustive list, but make sure that you are aware of these points as they affect you.

Finally, you may be sent the employment contract which refers to a number of rules within the Staff Handbook. This will give you additional information about the post and the company.

Assessing the offer

In your original analysis of your skills and your needs,
you will have assessed those factors in a job and/or the
organisation which are important to you. This gave
you your 'bottom line' on a number of elements. Once
you have received the offer of the post and understood
all that it entails, you should assess this against those
criteria you previously acknowledged were important.
If the job easily meets your needs, you have no
problem, but if you find that you are willing to accept
something less than you originally wanted, check your
motivation!

Try to be systematic about your analysis. You may
find that there are trade-offs, and that you are willing
to compromise on the salary in favour of certain career
prospects. There is of course, no reason why you
should not change your initial estimation to accept a
post (it's your life!) but make sure that you know what
you are doing and why.

You are now ready to take up the offer of the post
and begin your new job. Good luck!

Further reading

There are a number of books, handbooks and pamphlets which could help you with your job search and presentation. This chapter gives a small selection of some of the reading which can help you prepare. It is divided into sections so that you can focus on one particular area if you wish. Alternatively use the general reading section. Ask in your local bookshop or library, too, for any other useful information which they may have.

Company background

Extel cards
The Kompass Directory (Kompass Publishers)
Key British Enterprises (Dun & Bradstreet)
The Times 1000 (Times Publishing)
The Financial Times
With the newspapers, you will have to scan these for any stories about the organisation you are interested in. Most importantly, you should obtain any company literature that you can, including the annual report.

Careers guidance and applications

The first book listed is invaluable if you are contemplating a career change or just don't know where to start. It is very readable and helps you analyse your own skills and preferences.

The Careers Guide 1994/5, Diane Burston (Kogan Page)
Company Magazine Top 100 Jobs, Suzanne Askham (Vermillion)

How to Choose a Career, Vivien Donald (Kogan Page)
An A–Z of Careers and Jobs, Diane Burston (Kogan Page)
My job application (Hobson's Press)
Preparing your own CV, Rebecca Corfield (Kogan Page)
CV's and Written Applications, Judy Skeats (Ward Lock)
The Perfect Cover Letter, R.H. Beatty (John Wiley & Sons Ltd)
Guidance on specific careers is also available from many professional bodies, together with details of the required qualifications for entry to their examination schemes.

School/college leavers

The Job Book (Hobson's Press)
Graduate Employment and Training (Hobson's Press)
Directory of Opportunities for Graduates (VNU Business Publications Ltd)
Penguin careers guide, Anne Alston (Penguin)
Which subject? Which careers?, Alan Jamieson (Consumers' Association – Which? series)
There are numerous publications and guides for graduates and school leavers. Your librarian should be able to provide more information on these.

Women

Here is a small selection of the useful publications. Note that unions and University women's sections may also have helpful literature.
Getting There: Job Hunting for Women, Margaret Willis (Kogan Page)
Graduate Working Woman Casebook (Hobson's Press)

Part Time Work, Judith Humphries (Kogan Page)
Back to Work: A Practical Guide for Women, Cathy Moulder and Pat Shelton (Kogan Page)
Returners (National Advisory Centre on Careers for Women)
Overcoming the Career Break: a Positive Approach, Carole Truman (Manpower Services Commission)

Executives

Executives in Action, C. Moore (MacDonald & Evans)
How to succeed in a highly competitive job market, Brian Croucher (Kogan Page)
How to win at the job game, E.J. Parsons (Kogan Page)
The Executive Grapevine (Executive Grapevine Ltd)
A Guide to Executive Re-employment, Charles Dudeney (MacDonald & Evans)
Selling Yourself in the Management Market, John Courtis (British Institute of Management)
The last is particularly useful, full of tips.

Interviews

Interviews: How to Succeed, Judy Skeats (Ward Lock)
Answer the question, get the job, Iain Maitland (Centur Business)
The good interview guide, Susan Clemie (Rosters)
How to face interviewers, Clive Fletcher (Thorsons)
How to pass that interview, Judith Johnstone (How to Books)
Successful interview skills, Rebecca Corfield (Kogan Page)
How to be interviewed (Modus)
Get That Job!, Clive Fletcher (Thorsons)
Preparing for interviews, Shelley Burt (Pitman)

The books on interviewing above are guides on how to do it. Those in the section below are guides for interviewers, useful if you want to know what they are trying to achieve.

Effective Interviewing for Employment Selection, Clive T. Goodworth (Business Books)

The Interview Game and How it is Played, Celia Roberts (BBC)

General

How to Win Friends and Influence People, Dale Carnegie (Worlds Work)

Getting to Yes: Negotiating Agreement without Giving In, Roger Fisher and William Ury (Hutchinson)

Effective Presentation, Antony Jay (BIM)

(Although the latter does not directly consider interview techniques, many presentation techniques are similar and you would undoubtedly benefit from reading the parts on body language.)

A Woman in Your Own Right, Anne Dickson (Quartet Books)

(Not just for women, and gives a very good guide to assertion techniques which may help your interview performance.)

The IPM Recruitment Code (Institute of Personnel Management)

The latter is a small pamphlet giving a code of conduct which they recommend should be followed by employers and job seekers.